"David wrote in Psalm 25 [...] who fear Him; He will [...] Young is one to whom much of this knowledge has obviously been imparted. In The Covenant Keeper she invites us on a journey to share with us some of the depths and beauties regarding covenant which have been disclosed to her along the way. I found her book enlightening, at times deeply moving, and recommend it highly."

—**Martin Sarvis**, Succat Hallel (Tabernacle of Praise), Jerusalem

"Ruthie has a unique ability to dig through the scriptures and express the hidden treasures. As we read through this book we were able to understand and even visualize what happened and what was experienced as each covenant was made. In addition, the sections on the women of the Bible, the weddings and the feasts were very helpful in the understanding how God used each of these in His plan for where we are now."

—**Lonnie & Annette Lavender,** War Cry Prayer Ministry, Dennison, Texas

"Ruthie Young powerfully explores the depths of our relationship with God Almighty through the eyes of covenant language. Page after page will explode from the printed word to resonate the Truth and Love of the Father in your soul. Go beyond the veil and discover one of the most inspiring and insightful books about our God – The Covenant Keeper."

—**John Gowen**, Pastor, Cornerstone Christian Fellowship, Corinth, MS

"I've always had a desire for increased revelation in regard to covenant. After all, covenant is the very center and essence of God's plan for redeeming humanity, and it should stir something in us to search, to know, and to understand more. When I read Ruthie Young's book, which is replete with revelation and truth on this subject, I was able to embrace dimensions of covenant I had never experienced before. "From the beginning until the final page, I found my heart opening up and connecting to my Covenant Keeper in a whole new way. Ruthie uncovers this truth and paints a beautiful picture of His passion for His Bride, the Church, and the revealing of His covenant plan for her throughout the ages. I encourage you to read this amazing work and allow the Lord to open the way for you also to step into new and renewed levels of covenant with your Covenant Keeper!"

—**Charlotte Merschbrock**, Jubilee Destiny Ministries, Natchitoches, LA

"Step by step Ruthie Young will walk you through God's covenant with His people. Her book reveals not only how He keeps his covenant with us but how He helps us preserve our part of the covenant with Him. Page after page The Covenant Keeper brings to light how God's relationship with us is forever."

—**Peter McPheters**, Author, Corinth, MS

Blessings Luci,
He is Our Kinsman
Redeemer — our Covenant
Keeper —
     Love You,
     Ruthie
     Jer. 29:11

Covenant Keeper

Covenant Keeper

By

Ruthie Young

The Covenant Keeper

Copyright © 2018 by Mary Ruth Young

Unless otherwise indicated, Scripture quotations are taken from the New King James Version®. Copyright © 1982 by Thomas Nelson. Used by permission. All rights reserved.

Scripture quotations labeled MSG are taken from Scripture taken from The Message. Copyright © 1993, 1994, 1995, 1996, 2000, 2001, 2002. Used by permission of NavPress Publishing Group.

Scripture quotations labeled Voice are taken from The Voice™. Copyright © 2008 by Ecclesia Bible Society. Used by permission. All rights reserved.

Scripture quotations labeled GW are taken from Scripture are taken from GOD'S WORD®, © 1995 God's Word to the Nations. Used by permission of Baker Publishing Group.

Scripture quotations marked KJV are taken from the King James Version of the Bible.

All rights reserved. No part of this publication may be reproduced, stored in a retrieval system, or transmitted in any form or by any means—electronic, mechanical, photocopy, recording, or any other—except for brief quotations in printed reviews, without the prior permission of the author.

ISBN-13: 978-1722302993

ISBN-10: 1722302992

Cover design: James Nesbit, James Nesbit Art

Interior design: Phil and Erin Ulrich, Design by Insight

Edited by: Sandra Peoples, Next Step Editing; Mary Russell, Editor at Large

Contents

Acknowledgements and Thanks	9
Dedication	11
Foreword by James Nesbit	13
Foreword by Linda Heidler	15
Introduction	17
Prologue: The Foundation Stone of Blood Covenant	19
Chapter 1: Our Kinsman Redeemer, The Go'el	25
Chapter 2: Basic Truths of Covenant	29
Chapter 3: Specific Covenants	45
Chapter 4: The Law of the Kinsman Redeemer, the Go'el	65
Chapter 5: The Five Women in Matthew	85
Chapter 6: A Closer Look at Weddings	107
Chapter 7: The Covenant Feasts of the Kinsman Redeemer	119
Epilogue: Jesus, The Go'el, the Covenant Keeper	135

Acknowledgements and Thanks

I have had much prayer and assistance with this book and I want to thank all who prayed, edited, suggested, and helped me. Here are a few of you:

Martin Sarvis has been a valuable source of inspiration and assistance, particularly in the area of Hebrew words and information about the Feasts. Martin teaches Torah one day each week in Jerusalem at Succot Hallel. He is a dear friend and an excellent teacher. Thank you, Martin for all of your input and your wonderful, rich laugh! We love you and Norma.

My exceptional, awesome prayer team. Your faithfulness to pray for me over such a long time was amazing. You have sent me prophetic words and encouragement when I wanted to give up and set the atmosphere for me in prayer as I wrote. Your prayers are such a deep part of this book and my heart is so grateful to all of you. I don't think I could have made it without you. Thank you.

Charlotte Merschbrock, you have been my cheerleader, editor (eagle eye), encourager, and sounding board. Thank you.

My sisters and children, my support team throughout this process.

Sandra Peebles, my first editor, who was so helpful and patient with me as we struggled with the first edit. I pray your new book will be out soon!

And of course, Mary Russell, my friend and second editor. I have learned about sentence structure while enjoying rich fellowship and lots of laughs. Thank you.

Erin and Phil Ulrich. There is no way to express my thanks to you, my friends, as you patiently walked me through the publishing process, one step at the time. Thank you.

Dedication

This book is dedicated to the one who has been a covenant keeper for forty-seven years and counting. You have been there for me, willingly releasing me to disappear for days to write, picking up suppers when I couldn't take time to cook and even doing laundry. You are my soul mate, a wonderful life partner and have shown me in many ways what covenant looks like on "Monday morning." I love you, Billy Joe.

Foreword
by James Nesbit

I have known Billy Joe and Ruthie Young for a dozen years or more, and have been on several prayer journeys with them. The one thing they exemplify above all else as a couple is covenant. So, for Ruthie to be one that Father has chosen to expand our understanding of covenant is a glorious choice indeed!

Ruthie is a gold miner, she mines nuggets from the depths of the riches of Christ and polishes them with the beauty of her unique perspective that opens dimensions of thought and releases new realms of light and understanding of our Covenant Keeping God, Go'el, our kinsman redeemer.

Ruthie is a southern belle and a wonderful story teller. I just love to hear her tell her stories with that Mississippi accent. As I was reading this book, I could feel the warmth of her heart and could hear whispers of her accent singing from the pages, as she magnifies the beauty of the lover of our soul. It was like I had the privilege of sitting in on a conversation with her grandchildren as she was giving them a gift they would cherish through eternity.

We are living in the hour when the Covenant Keeper is remembering the covenants that he has made with our forebears, who called upon His Name long ago! Yes, we have stepped into the era of the fullness of the promise, and this book will help position you to receive all that Father has for you, your bloodline, and your family tree.

A Note from Dr. Chuck D. Pierce

As you know, I am a huge champion of women in ministry. The minute I saw *The Covenant Keeper* by Ruthie Young, I knew I was to pass it on to one of the best women ministers I know, Linda Heidler. Linda herself has a new book on women that is near completion. Following are her comments that will help you enter into the power of covenant relationship with *Yeshua*, our Savior and Redeemer.

Foreword by Linda Heidler

I have known Ruthie Young for a number of years. During that time, I have watched her go through the hardship of her husband being in a life threatening automobile accident, the long process of recovery, and the decision to let go of one way of ministry in order to transition a different way of ministry. All of these are potentially devastating experiences. Many do not recover from events like these. Yet, through all of it, her faith did not falter and she emerged stronger and with increased confidence in who she was and what she was to do. She could only have done this through an understanding and experience of what it means to live in covenant with God. What Ruthie writes in *The Covenant Keeper* could only have come from firsthand experience with a covenant keeping God.

In this book, Ruthie delves into the multifaceted nature of covenant. Beginning with the foundation of covenant in blood sacrifice, she unfolds one aspect of covenant after another, bringing revelation to the beauty and the depth of God's covenant with us. The way that each covenant God made with man built on the previous one shows the eternal plan of God for the redemption of man. The loyalty of the Kinsman Redeemer is a beautiful foretelling of Jesus, our Kinsman Redeemer. The experiences of the five women included in Matthew's genealogy of Jesus gives a picture of how personal God intends His covenant with us to be. The covenant symbolism found in weddings, particularly in Jewish wedding ceremonies, brings a new perspective on the covenant of marriage. The revelation in each of the Biblical feasts shows the desire of God to remind us of His covenant as we celebrate these year by year. Finally, she presents the revelation of Jesus as our Kinsman Redeemer, the one through whom covenant is secured.

There is much to contemplate in this book. There are many things to meditate on to let the depth of the revelation sink in. There are truths that will bring security, peace, confidence, and faith into your daily life. These are all things Ruthie possesses because of her assurance of her covenant with God. We will all benefit from coming into the revelation and experience of covenant as presented in this book. It is not meant to be read just to gain knowledge or understanding, but to bring us into living in the blessing of our covenant with God, the true "Covenant Keeper."

Introduction
The Covenant Keeper, The Go'el

Years ago as a young Christian, I was asked to lead worship at a ladies' retreat. The teacher spoke about the details of God's covenant with Abraham and my heart was captured by the idea of covenant. I began a quest for more knowledge and understanding of His covenant with me. Studying the covenants in the Old Testament, I realized the different accounts from Adam to Moses to David were all expansions of only one true covenant. The intensity and language grew with each sequential story of covenant, enlarging the beauty, perception, character, and responsibility of Jehovah, the covenant-keeping God.

Of course, there is always more to discover and know about the covenant, but as the years went by, there seemed to be a strategic portion, a missing part, I had not discovered. In 2011, God answered that longing deep in my heart with a gift for me at Christmas, when our pastor, John Gowen, taught about the Hebrew word *go'el*, the Kinsman Redeemer. This name exploded in my spirit and resonated in my heart as the missing piece. I had read about the kinsman redeemer in the book of Ruth but had never grasped the depth and the essence of God from the perspective of the *Go'el* until that Christmas in 2011. Never before had I seen how it is repeated in story after story in the Bible. This Kinsman Redeemer, our *Go'el*, is so much more than I had ever thought or imagined. Now I find Him throughout the Bible as the initiator and keeper of the covenant.

The Covenant Keeper, the *Go'el*.

Prologue

The Foundation Stone of Blood Covenant

The Book of First Peter states that Jesus was crucified before the foundation of the earth. What would that look like? How did this come to be? We do not have that information.

I am a visionary learner. If I can see it I have a better grasp of the information given. As I pondered the statement, "Before the foundation of the earth." I began to visualize a possible scenario and conversation between the Father, Son, and Holy Spirit.

The following drama is how I imagined it could have been. Please go with me into eternity before time was created. A place when the three in one, Elohim existed alone, without another like Himself. There were angels there because Ezekiel tells us that Lucifer had fallen long before the earth was created and had taken with Him one third of the angelic realm. Job declared that the Morning Stars, possibly angelic beings, sang when He pulled the land up from the deep waters, yet the galaxies were not created until the fourth day. As an integral part of His being, light and worship were present. And yet, a heart deeper than any ocean and wider than any sky yearned for an Other like Himself. His desire was for a bride.

Before the Beginning

In the vast nothingness, chaos reigned as Elohim hovered over the dark waters of disarray and confusion. The only sound heard or felt was the deep cry of a lonely heart yearning for His Other. This Other would complete His joy, receive His kindness, and echo back His love. Pure love must be given away freely or it is not love at all. And love without an object to receive it is really quite meaningless. Pure love is what made this mysterious community of Father, Son, and Spirit truly one God—Elohim.

In the profound intensity of this yearning, Elohim conceived a plan. He would make an Other in His own likeness. Lovely and creative, she would know life in the fullest sense. She would be like Him -- spirit, soul, and body, male and female. She would dream, she would know joy, and yes, she would know sorrow.

As He visualized His plan unfolding, He recognized His old adversary Lucifer would be standing by yet again ready to steal, kill, and destroy any object of His love.

Oh, but she would love Him back, wouldn't she? Surely she would always choose Him. But love without choice is not love either. Love must be freely given and freely received or it becomes bondage, and bondage can never be described as love. She must be free to choose.

As He pondered this vision, end and beginning, with a broken heart He knew what her choice would be. He knew the beguiling lies of the Father of Lies would be too strong for her and would draw her away, bringing her into bondage and stealing her destiny, the destiny of becoming His bride, His Other.

No! That must never happen. He knew, even before she came to be, He must find a way back for her: a way for Him to catch her should she fall, a way to set her free should she become enslaved, a way to bring her back should she face the horror of hell and death. He must find a way.

So the conversation began within this mysterious community of One.

The Father spoke to His Beloved Son, "I know the yearning of your heart for an Other and I have envisioned for you a worthy, noble bride to fulfill the deep, burning desire of your heart."

Prologue

Catching the vision from His Father and with great joy and expectancy the Son declared, "Oh, Father, she is altogether lovely. One glance from her eyes and My heart will be captivated forever."

With deep anguish the Father spoke again. "But alas, I also see that our old adversary Lucifer will come to steal her heart with his mesmerizing voice and bewitching lies. She will listen to him, choose to believe him, and go with him. And there she will be wounded unto death. He will put shackles on her ankles and will veil her eyes so she cannot see clearly. He will cause her to believe she is beyond repair and no longer beautiful to us. Our enemy will take everything from her: her dignity, her honor, and her destiny—especially her destiny. He will cover her with shame, bringing her as a slave into his realm of death, hell, and the grave.

With a burning zeal, the Son spoke again to His Father, "But I will buy her back from this slavery, though it cost Me all I have, though it cost Me My very life. My glory, My riches, and My honor are meaningless without her."

With fervency the Son continued, "I have a plan. I will take her into the wilderness and pursue her. I will take the shackles off her feet so she can run with Me over the mountains. I will heal her wounds with the ointment of My love and I will lift her head so she may see herself reflected in My eyes: pure and spotless, clothed in restored glory, honor, and dignity."

The Spirit of Wisdom and Truth slowly rose to speak. A holy hush descended over all of eternity. Like the roar of many waters resonating throughout the heavens He spoke. "From the deepest treasures of eternity I bring forth the sacred truth. It is a truth too deep for our adversary Lucifer to perceive or fathom. This truth exists only in Our knowledge: The Truth of the Blood Covenant."

Deafening silence continued as all of heaven stood still to listen. This was a strange and unfathomable truth that had never been spoken throughout the ages of eternity.

Wisdom and Truth solemnly proceeded, "This covenant must be sealed with pure, holy blood at the altar known as the mercy seat behind the veil of holiness. Here at this holiest place in the throne room, You must bind Yourself to her through the irrevocable oath of the covenant, sealed with Your own blood. It is at this altar You will marry her and invoke the Law of the *Go'el* to redeem her as her Kinsman. You will take vengeance on her enemy as her Blood Avenger, buy her back from slavery, restoring her inheritance as her Redeemer, and reinstate her destiny as her Husband.

"But first, know these two truths. It is imperative that You go freely of Your Own choice, otherwise the authority will be lost. And just as vital, she must always have the freedom to choose."

A roar like that of a lion filled the heavens, ringing out over created time and echoing into eternity. With great joy the Son shouted, "And on Our wedding day she will be Mine again! Our adversary will be cast down forever and she will sit by My side reflecting all of My glory. Because of My great love for her, she will choose Me forever."

Then the Three as One, Elohim, understanding the exorbitant price to be paid, agreed that this was the only way. Together, the Father with a heavy heart and the Son with the glint of burning passion in His eye, slowly walked to the ancient stone altar to meet the Spirit of Wisdom and Truth. There, at the mercy seat, the Son took the oath of the covenant and was crucified from the foundation of the earth.

As His pure, holy blood streamed down the sides of the ancient altar stone, the ruach, the very breath of the Father thundered, "Let there be light!" and the song of creation and redemption came to be.*

Prologue

I have set you as an unbreakable seal upon My heart and upon My arm. My love for you is as strong as death itself and My burning zeal for you is as relentless as the grave. Torrential floods of water cannot quench the fire of My love for you, My sister, My bride. (Song of Sol. 8:6-7, paraphrased)

For You were bought with a price.

*Again, this is simply my own version of the statement: "Before the foundation of the earth."

Chapter One
Our Kinsman Redeemer, Our Go'el

Our God, Jehovah *Elohim*, the self-existent supreme one, has relentlessly pursued us since the beginning of all creation. He has meticulously painted pictures of His character so we might see His magnificence, His holiness, and His strength. His name has power precisely because it embodies His presence, His life, His nature. He longs for us to know Him for His glorious loving kindness, His tender mercy, His goodness, and His justice. While all of this is important, the utmost cry of His heart is for us to know Him as our Bridegroom, our Redeemer, the Lover of our soul.

Desperate situations call for desperate measures. There is no situation more desperate than the widowhood of all creation, (explained in greater depth later) which includes you, my friend. And it includes me. And there is no greater, higher nor deeper solution than the original Blood Covenant. This is the price of our redemption.

Covenant is gruesome. Covenant is bloody. But above all, covenant is holy. He created us to be His pure spotless bride. Then He paid the ultimate bride price to buy us back, to redeem us in our widowhood, to re-clothe us again as His bride. He is the Kinsman Redeemer. He is the Covenant Maker. And He is the Covenant Keeper.

He is *Elohim*, the Supreme Magistrate; *El Elyon*, the Most High God; Jehovah *Sabaoth*, the Commander of the angel armies. When we speak His name, He is Jehovah *Shammah*, the ever present with us; Jehovah *Tsidkenu*, the God who makes everything right; Jehovah *Ro-eh*, our Shepherd who cares for us and supplies all of our needs. These are just a few of His covenant names which release the power essential to pay our ransom, to avenge our injustice, to deliver us into freedom, and ultimately to marry us, bringing us into our full inheritance as His bride, intimately loving us eternally. It was for this we were created. It was for this we were redeemed. This is our destiny. We are His "Other."

From the beginning in Genesis, we were destined for the wedding ceremony of the Lamb in Revelation. We were created to be His bride, but as His bride we required redemption. We had to be pure and spotless, bought back from the slavery of death. We needed justice, mercy, and vindication. We needed an avenue to receive our full inheritance. We needed a *Go'el*, a Kinsman Redeemer.

According to *Strong's Concordance* (H1350) the *go'el* comes from a primitive root, *ga'al* meaning:

- To redeem
- To be the next of kin
- To buy back a relative's property
- To marry his widow
- To be a blood avenger; to bring justice
- To deliver
- To perform the part of near or next of kin
- To purchase or ransom

Although the Law of the *Go'el* or Kinsman Redeemer is first mentioned in Exodus 6:5-9, this name is one of the foundation stones of the covenant. From the beginning our Creator saw the end and knew a redeemer would be necessary for us to be His pure and spotless bride. Usually when we hear these words, "kinsman redeemer," we think of the story of Ruth, which is a beautiful picture of a kinsman redeemer, a picture of Jesus, ever wooing His bride. Yet throughout the Bible from Genesis to Revelation, an even deeper beauty, hope, and understanding of His covenant is hidden in the Hebrew name *go'el*.

A stirring picture of His relentless love for us comes from Hosea.

> "She got dressed up in her rings and jewelry; she went after her lovers; she forgot about Me. But once she has nothing, I'll be able to get through to her. I'll entice her and lead her out into the wilderness where we can be alone, and I'll speak right to her heart and try to win her back. And then I'll give her back her vineyards, I'll turn the Valley of Achor, (that is, "Valley of Trouble,") into a gateway of hope. In the wilderness of exile she'll learn to respond to Me the way she did when she was young when I brought her out of Egypt. And I swear when that day comes, she'll call me "My husband" and never address Me again as "My master." (Hosea 2:14-16, Voice)

He joyously pursues us, covers us, and purchases us. He who buys us back, pays all our debts, avenges our injustice, delivers us into freedom, pays our ransom, and plans to marry us. Described in detail throughout the Bible, Old and New Covenant, we see this amazing, beautiful picture played out in history. As our Kinsman Redeemer, He brings us into our full inheritance as His bride. As His bride we are loved eternally.

Key within the concept of blood covenant is the word atonement which means "to cover." We see our need for this reflected throughout the Bible. When Adam and Eve sinned, the glory was gone and they were uncovered. Jehovah killed an animal, possibly a lamb, and covered them. Boaz covered Ruth with his *tallit*. David was covered under the wings of the Almighty. Within each of us there is a deep fear of being exposed, vulnerable, and uncovered. We have a basic need to know we are hidden, safe, protected, and confident. Knowing this, the first action of the *go'el* is to cover us. Our *Go'el*, Jesus, was uncovered on the cross so we might be covered for all eternity. In Revelation at the Wedding Feast of the Lamb we see the bride once again covered with the light of His glory, full restoration of her inheritance lost in the garden.

Join me as we begin in Genesis with Adam and Eve. We will explore the different narratives of His covenant with Abraham, Moses and the children of Israel, and Jonathan and David. Then we will delve deeper into the beauty and holiness of our Kinsman Redeemer as portrayed in the lives of the five women noted in the genealogy of Jesus from the book of Matthew.

Finally we will look intently at Jesus Christ, our Kinsman Redeemer, our *Go'el*, as He came to buy us back from the darkness of our sin, to avenge our injustice, to right our wrong and to provide for us. He came to cover us when we are exposed, afraid and destitute. Jesus, our Kinsman Redeemer. Our *Go'el*.

Chapter Two
Basic Truths of Covenant

Covenant is God's answer to an impossible situation. As The Spirit brooded over the waters in Genesis one, He visualized all of creation, the end from the beginning. In the midst of longing to love and be loved by a people created in His own image, a bride for His Son, our great Creator possibly felt both joy and sorrow. Yet as a holy God, He knew our sin, our disobedience, would separate us forever from fellowship and relationship with Him, the very purpose for which we were created. He was totally aware of His enemy's plan to come and kill, steal, and destroy His precious children. His noble heart was torn because He also knew the price for their redemption: the suffering and death of His own beloved Son. Hebrews and First Peter both tell us Jesus Christ was slain from the foundation of the world. In deepest sorrow yet holiest joy, Abba Father found a way: covenant.

Jesus brought the beauty, the incredible promises, and the father heart of God into the New Covenant by fulfilling every portion of the Old Covenant. He stepped into covenant, became the covenant sacrifice and opened the door for all of the promises of the covenant to be released into the earth. He did not do away with the old but was methodically and precisely fulfilling each detail of the old in order to bring forth the new. This opened the door for the fullness of covenant to be released to all of creation, including the Gentiles. Jesus made it clear He came to the Jews first, but by fulfilling the stipulations of the Abrahamic covenant which said all nations would be blessed, He opened the door for all nations to come in.

Because Jesus completed the conditions of the Old Covenant, we can now live, move, and have our being in the fullness of the promises in His New Covenant.

"For all the promises of God in Him are yes and in Him Amen, to the glory of God through us." (II Corinthians 1:20)

Some Basic Truths of Covenant

God's covenant is unbreakable and is offered to us by grace. We are saved, not by an intellectual or emotional agreement, but by a covenantal commitment from God Himself. In our culture we work with contracts rather than covenants and there is a huge difference between the two.

A covenant is more than a promise, it is a formal, solemn, binding agreement written and sealed between two or more parties for the performance of some action. Covenants are based on trust and cannot be broken without cost of life. The language of covenant is "until death do we part" and can even extend to the next generation. Ancient covenants included words like loyalty, faithfulness, and allegiance. God's covenants are eternal. The word covenant is first mentioned in Gen 6:18 with Noah. But as we look at the terms and requirements of God's covenant, we see God made a covenant with us at the foundation of the world when Jesus was sacrificed.

A contract, on the other hand, is based on distrust and can be dissolved if both parties agree to dissolve it. The language in a contract utilizes words such as "if broken," "When this is finished," and "If the person does this, then …" It is also limited to time. In our society, we are much more familiar with a contract than a covenant, which is a sad commentary on us.

In the book of Jeremiah God makes clear His idea of covenant. "Thus says the Lord: 'If you can break my covenant with the day and my covenant with the night, so that there will not be day and night in their season, then my covenant may also be broken...'" (Jeremiah 33:20-21).

I'd like to share a personal story about that particular Scripture. In 2014, my husband was in a serious auto accident. He sustained nine broken ribs, a broken sternum, both arms in casts, and spent six days in the intensive care unit of the hospital. Needless to say, I was a little overwhelmed with what our life looked like the first day home from the hospital. Our daughter Aly'ce had come to stay with us and her eight-year-old son Wesley came with her, bringing his new bike. After very little sleep and much trauma, I could hardly think straight. Early that first morning Wesley was eager for the two of us to go outside so I could observe his skill of riding his shiny new bicycle. I was pretty numb emotionally and watching Wesley ride on this crisp October morning brought a smile to my heart. As I was enjoying the fresh air I heard the Lord say, "Look up!" So I did. I looked up into the full brightness of the sun. With a chuckle in His voice He whispered, "The sun came up today." What a strange statement from the Lord to my heart! What in the world did it mean to me? Suddenly Jeremiah 33 came crashing into my mind. I was flooded with warmth, joy, and a feeling of safety. I felt covered. I laughed, cried, and danced in the street! "As long as the sun rises and sets and the night follows day, so is my covenant with you, Ruthie. It can never be broken. I will never leave you nor forsake you." Gone was the huge lump I had carried during the previous week. Gone was the heavy burden of looming decisions. I was totally surprised by His joy, His love and His comfort. God had kept His covenant with the day and night, and surely He would keep His covenant with me. "The sun came up today!"

The Hebrew word for covenant is *berith* literally meaning "cutting the flesh" and comes from two words which mean "the work of Jah" and "to create, to cut, select or choose" (*Strong's Concordance*, #1285, #1262, #1254). In other words, Jehovah *Elohim*, the most vehemently holy, self-existent God, King of the universe, chose to cut a covenant with us. Knowing we could never keep our part of this covenant, which meant certain death, He chose to fulfil both parts of the covenant at the cost of His own life. Becoming flesh, He died in our place.

Cutting a covenant was not an uncommon thing to do in the early cultures of the Middle East. According to *Eerdmans' Handbook to the Bible*, this custom is noted in the historic accounts of ancient tribes such as the Hittites. There the tenets and stipulations of the covenant ceremony, along with the feast that always followed, are recorded. Genesis 15 and Jeremiah 34 both refer to the ancient covenant ceremony of cutting and dividing animals into two parts. As the covenanting parties walked between the pieces of the animals, in essence they were saying, "May I be torn apart like these animals if I fail to uphold my part of this covenant." In the Genesis account of Jehovah's covenant with Abram, God alone passes between the slaughtered animals while Abram slept, emphasizing again His solemn, solitary, and ultimate level of commitment involved in this covenant.

As these covenants were made, there was always a written agreement or document of the terms of the covenant. Interestingly the Greek word that we translate "testament" is in reality the word covenant. Therefore, what we recognize as our Bible today is simply the description, terms, agreements, and fulfillment of Jehovah's covenant with us, ever expanding from the old and completed in the new.

The Tenets of Covenant

Looking a little deeper into the ancient history of the Hittite era, we discover that covenants were fairly common in Northern Africa and the Middle East. Historically there were seven parts of the covenant recognized by the people of the day. They were:

- The preamble identifying the parties involved, which always included their god or gods
- The prologue describing the relationship of the parties involved

- The stipulations or responsibilities of both parties
- The blessings and curses of obedience or disobedience
- The succession arrangement as to how this would be passed on generationally
- The actual cutting of flesh
- A feast which usually lasted for seven days

Seven is precious to the Lord. The Hebrew word for oath literally means "To seven one's self to another." It is the number of completion and perfection. From the seven days of creation to the seven churches in Revelation, seven is found 735 times in our Bible. There are seven days in one week and the seventh day is set aside for the Lord as Sabbath. The seventh day is the first instance of anything being sanctified and set aside as holy to the Lord. It is interesting to note that the Sabbath was set aside for intimate fellowship with the Lord and the seventh portion of the covenant ceremony is a feast to celebrate with joy and fellowship. Again-completion and perfection.

The ancient covenants began with the preamble. This portion named the initiator and author of the covenant, who was usually the one with more wealth and authority. Throughout the New Testament Jesus continually reminds us it is the Father calling us to come: "No one can come to Me unless the Father who sent Me draws him" (John 6:44). Just as the shepherd seeks his sheep, so the Father longs for us to come to Him and walk in covenant with Him. Without a doubt the Father is the initiator of our covenant.

Because the written document of covenant was to be read on a yearly basis, scribes were present to write every word spoken during the ceremony. These writers insisted on revealing the grace and mercy of the initiator. Words such as "go after," "love," "hearken to the voice calling" were used to stir up the emotions of the two parties making covenant. This language revealed it would be more than a mere contract or intellectual agreement; this level of commitment required feeling, sentiment, and invoked a response of loyalty, faithfulness, and allegiance toward the initiator of the covenant.

The preamble also listed all of the assets of both parties of the covenant. Recognizing the assets of the greater party gave confidence to the lessor party that the land owner or king had the resources available to meet the requirements of provision and protection for the lessor party.

In Abram's case as in ours, the King of the Universe, Jehovah *Elohim* is the author and initiator of the covenant. Throughout our covenant book, the Bible, Jehovah's attributes and assets are identified and recorded. He is the King of the universe, Creator of all mankind, the God of all flesh. His riches include, but are not limited to, all of the cattle on a thousand hills and all of the sliver and gold in the earth. In fact Psalm 24 declares that the entire earth belongs to Him. We are assured time and again, our God has sufficient assets to meet the requirements of provision and redemption for us. We are promised that when we call on Lord Sabaoth, commander of the hosts of heaven, the God of the angel armies, He is fully equipped, armed, and well able to come to our aid and rescue.

Next came the historical prologue. Prior to the cutting of covenant, the prologue defined the relationship of the parties: landowner and his tenants, two kings or even two friends of equal rank. The cutting of covenant shifted their relationship. If the two parties were of equal rank, the relationship became as brother to brother. However, if there was a greater party, such as a land owner to his tenants, the relationship became as father to son. Most covenants were cut between a greater party and a lesser party. Obviously God is the greater party in His covenant with us. In realizing that Jehovah *Elohim*, supreme Ruler of the universe, would choose to enter a covenant with me, the lesser party, I am both humbled and awestruck.

Throughout our Bible the Lord says, "I will be your Husband. I will be your Father." The words "I will" do not simply mean "I intend to do a thing." These are covenant words based on an oath of blood, which means, "I will complete all that I swear to do, even at the cost of my own life. I will seven myself to you."

As the stipulations were explained, the mutual responsibilities of the partners were disclosed. For instance, the landowner pledged to provide for the welfare and protection of his tenants, while the tenants pledged to work the land and give service to the landlord.

On the other hand, if a covenant was made between people of equal authority such as two kings, the stipulations were quite different. These covenants were on a much higher level. A covenant such as this would include an oath not to invade the other's territory and to come to the aid of the other quickly in times of war, hardship, or lack. They swore to respect each other with fair trade agreements and such. This type covenant was binding until death and sometimes included future generations. In essence they agreed to honor each other as brothers.

Our covenant was the former -- Jehovah initiated the covenant as our Father and Jesus took our place as our Brother.

Along with this binding agreement there was a prerequisite for the covenanters to remember and renew these vows at regular intervals, usually at the same time once a year. God commanded the Israelites to appear before Him three times a year to remember and celebrate *Pesach*/Passover in the early spring, *Shavuot*/Pentecost fifty days later, and *Sukkot*/Tabernacles in the fall.

The first three feasts celebrated in the spring commemorated their release from Egypt with Passover, Unleavened Bread, and First Fruits. It was during these feasts Jesus actually cut covenant with us in the flesh, was buried, and raised as the first fruit of resurrection. Fifty days later came the fourth feast of *Shavuot* or Pentecost, celebrating the gift of Torah at Mt. Sinai. At this feast Jesus gave the gift of the Holy Spirit to the new believers. The fifth, sixth, and seventh feasts came in the fall with the Feast of Trumpets, *Yom Kippur* or Day of Atonement, followed by the seven-day Feast of Tabernacles or *Sukkot*, a time of great fellowship and joy. During these fall feasts, we as believers look forward to Jesus' return and the celebration of the Wedding Feast of the Lamb.

It was not uncommon during ancient times for people to worship many gods, some personal, some national. A list of gods, noted by name in the covenant testimony, were called upon to witness the covenant. Well aware of the spiritual dimension, these people knew that entering into this covenant involved the unseen world with possible spiritual consequences if their gods were displeased.

Over and over the Lord said to His people, "I am Jehovah, your God. There is no other God but Me. You shall worship no other gods before Me" (Exodus 20:4). Jesus spoke of being the only door, the only way, the truth, and the life. He is the only way by which men can be saved. Our covenant testimony, the Bible, reminds us that, yes, there is an unseen world, and yes, this covenant does involve much spiritual interaction and consequence. But clearly the only God involved in our covenant is our one true God, Jehovah *Elohim*, and we worship Him alone.

A recording of the curses and the blessings followed, threatening the lesser party with illness or death if he broke the covenant, but promising him prosperity and blessing if he remained faithful. God's covenant testimony, Torah, plainly lays out the blessings and the curses in Deuteronomy 28 as God made covenant with the Israelites. By His blood we know Jesus broke the curses for us and we live under the blessing of His grace, poured out abundantly on us. However, if we purposefully choose to walk away from our covenant, we lose His protection and our rebellion opens the door for disastrous results.

All of these tenets -- the preamble, relationship, the names of the gods and the blessings and curses-were written down and kept by each party. This testimony was treasured and could be legally enforced if the stipulations were not fulfilled, even to the sentence of death. It was stored in a place of honor in their homes as a reminder of the covenant, their legal access to the benefits of the covenant promises, and their responsibility for what they had pledged in return. This testimony was to be read aloud and celebrated each year, renewing it from generation to generation. Traditionally the Jewish people read the Torah aloud when they celebrate the Feast of *Shavuot*/Pentecost.

This document was seen as an oath of life or death depending on the heart of the individual. If they intended to keep all of the rules and requirements, then they could walk in the peace of provision and protection. However, if their heart and actions were toward rebellion, death could come swiftly.

The succession arrangements were clearly stated as to how the benefits and relationship of the covenant would be passed on to the next generation. A cut on the hand was man-to-man, one generation, as a brother to brother relationship. However, if the covenant was to be generational, normally they made a cut on the inside of their thigh. In Genesis when Abraham's servant promised to bring back a bride for Isaac, he grasped the inside of Abraham's thigh as a sign of covenant oath to follow through with his promise, even at the cost of his life.

Obviously God's covenant with Abraham was generational. When Jehovah cut covenant with him, Abraham was commanded to circumcise himself and the men of his household. The cut of circumcision meant that Abraham's seed would always pass through the cut, the sign of the covenant. As this sign passed from generation to generation, blood was shed, and each cut represented renewal of the covenant, which continues today. That is why it is such an important ceremony when a Jewish baby boy is circumcised. This baby boy is literally cutting covenant with *El Elyon*, the King of the Universe. And the King of the Universe sees and remembers too.

When Constantine wanted to distance the early church from their Jewish roots, two of the first things to go were celebrating Sabbath and circumcision. He made it against the law for Jews and believers alike to celebrate these important remembrances of their ancient covenant. Since Messianic believers understood the importance of their generational covenant, they chose to face death rather than do away with celebrating Sabbath, the Feasts and other tenets of the Abrahamic Covenant.

Each year the testimony was to be brought out with great ceremony and read aloud with all parties present. Verbally renewing the vows of covenant, the early Hittites sacrificed an animal again to remember the shedding of blood and celebrated with a joyous feast.

We believers, still do this when we set aside memorial days, anniversaries, and holidays. We celebrate Resurrection Day (Easter) to remember when Jesus cut covenant with us through His sacrifice on the cross and His resurrection. Many churches today add a Seder celebration, the meal of remembrance from the Jewish Passover. It was at Passover when Jesus literally cut a covenant with us. As He shared the wine and the bread at His last Seder meal He used covenant language when He instructed them, "Do this in remembrance of me" (Luke 22:19). Because this covenant meal was so strategic and vital to our redemption I have written in much more detail about this solemn occasion later in this book.

The reading of the testimony was just the prologue to the most sobering component of the entire ceremony. The actual cutting of covenant.

Visualize two kings, both of great nations, dressed in their regal attire, making covenant with each other.

Meeting at the borders of their respective lands, they built an altar of stone and a fire from the wood they had each brought to the ceremony.

They each brought a sheep or goat from their own fold for the sacrifice. This animal would take on the fullness of identity of the individual king from which it came.

The kings, not their servants, slaughtered their own animal, allowing the blood to flow freely onto the ground. As they sliced these bloody animals into pieces, their royal robes became soaked in the carnage and filth of the sacrifice. Not a pretty sight. This was a labor-intensive task, but one that was required by the covenant nevertheless.

Laying out the pieces of raw, bloody meat, sandals soiled and robes dripping, they walked the blood path together, each solemn step a reminder of the vows being made: "If I do not keep this vow, this will be my blood being spilled on the ground."

As Jehovah cut covenant with Abram in this manner and walked twice between the pieces of the sacrifice, was He looking ahead to yet another blood path? Could He see the blood path His Son would walk as He struggled to drag the heavy cross down the Via Dolorosa, the Way of Suffering? Did His Father Heart grieve as He visualized His Son's bloody footprints in the dust on His way to Calvary? Yes. I believe He did.

During these poignant moments, God alone passed between the slaughtered animals while Abram slept, again emphasizing His solemn, solitary, and ultimate level of commitment—God putting His very life on the line for us. Our gracious Father knew that for Abram to walk this blood path would be certain death. Abram, nor any other man save one, could ever keep the vows being made that day.

Back to our kings: As they took a portion of the sacrificed animals, usually the right thigh, and laid it on the burning altar, the fragrance of burning flesh filled the atmosphere. This smell was a statement of death to their former identities. You see, covenant has a fragrance: it smells like burning flesh. On this day everything would change. On this day they became one.

Each taking a portion of their own sacrificed animal and feeding it to the other, they declared, "This is my flesh. As you eat my flesh, you and I become one."

Then, each brought their best wine, poured it into one cup, mixed it before the altar of sacrifice. Taking a sharp knife, they cut themselves on the hand or wrist and dripped some of their own blood into the cup of mixed wine. Placing their bloody hands together, they raised this cup and shouted, "This cup is my blood. This is the cup of our covenant!" and they both drank from the cup until it was finished.

At this point, they each embraced their new identity. They exchanged robes declaring, "My possessions are now yours." They exchanged weapons with the understanding that your enemies are now my enemies.

As they made the cut, usually on the hand, wrist, or even a circle around the thumb as a ring, they took ashes from the sacrificial fire and put them into the wound, insuring there would be a visible scar, a reminder of their covenant with each other until death.

This very scar could be used as a weapon of war. As other nations or kings came out to fight, this leader would show his scar and the opposing king would know immediately that this was a covenant sign. He would be aware that he would have to fight not only this particular king, but also the king with whom he was in covenant. Many times their enemy would be turned back because of this scar.

Does that sound familiar? In Isaiah, God says, "I will engrave you on the palm of my hand, you are mine." Jesus cut a covenant with us on the cross. You are literally engraved on the palm of His hand. When He sees His scars, He remembers you. As your enemies come against you and you call out to Jesus your covenant partner, He comes quickly to your aid. The principalities and powers tremble and are turned away, not only because of His power and His might, but they also see your name engraved on His hand. They, too, understand this covenant sign.

Jesus always spoke covenant language. "He who eats My flesh and drinks My blood abides in Me, and I in him." According to John 6:56, many followers left the day He spoke those words. They left because they understood covenant language and knew what Jesus was asking of them. Perhaps they wondered what this itinerant preacher had to offer them? They saw He had nothing on earth to give, and they knew that in a covenant all they had would be at His disposal. Perhaps they were suspicious that His enemies were on the rise and they certainly did not want to have to fight against the Pharisees, or worse, the Romans. They did not realize He was offering them His

Kingdom. He was extending an invitation to bring transformation to the world in which they lived. They could not see that the King of the Universe was offering them His riches in glory. Understanding the commitment of covenant, but being blinded to His true identity, they walked away from the greatest opportunity ever offered to mankind, the opportunity to cut covenant with the Son of the Most High, *El Elyon*. I wonder if I had been in that crowd, would I have turned away, too? I don't know. I do know just as they did, covenants are not to be entered into lightly. A few stayed. I pray I would have been one of those.

As Jesus raised the unleavened bread on His last Passover evening, He was preparing to cut covenant with us. "This is my body, broken for you." Did they understand? Taking the cup He said to His friends, "This is my blood, the blood of the new covenant." The Bible tells us that for the joy set before Him, He endured the cross. Just as Jehovah alone walked the blood path for Abraham, Jesus knew that He alone, must walk the blood path of eternity for us. His blood alone would be shed on the cross in the coming morning. What was this joy that gave Him the courage, the strength to walk through the next twenty-four hours of suffering? His return to His father? Yes. But I believe there was more. It was you. It was your face, your freedom, your redemption as His bride that gave Him strength. He had created you and now He would buy you back as your Kinsman Redeemer, your *Go'el*. He was preparing to cut covenant with you.

The covenant ceremony always ended with a joyous feast that usually lasted for seven days with plenty to eat and drink. God loves to eat and drink with His kids. He had lunch with Abraham. During the giving of the covenant testimony, the Torah, He invited Moses and the elders of Israel up to His formal dining hall where the floor was made of sapphire, and they enjoyed a grand banquet. Jesus ate and drank with His friends, the sinners, and the tax collectors. Appearing on the shore of the Sea of Galilee after His resurrection, He prepared breakfast for His disciples and ate with them.

Breaking bread together is a strategic part of the covenant. When we have a meal with someone, our relationship shifts to a new level. There is an openness that comes; a deeper fellowship evolves. That is God's plan, to eat and drink with His people. He established feasts for that purpose, to fellowship with His covenant family. Interestingly, the last chapter in our covenant book describes the Wedding Feast of the Lamb, bringing the covenant full circle.

In a contract we sign a paper and can walk away. But covenant always ends with a celebration of relationship, sealed with the shedding of blood, and the sharing of a meal.

My friend Charlotte Merschbrock wrote a blog post about this very thing. Here is a portion of what she wrote:

> Gatherings at a family table can build up and strengthen each member for His work and destiny. Jesus used food and mealtimes as the backdrop for some of His greatest miracles, teachings, and revelations.
>
> He miraculously fed the 5000 and then the 4000—you know the story of how He started with minimal provision and ended with baskets and baskets of leftovers. (See, it's OK to serve and eat leftovers!) Then it was at a meal (Passover) He shared the New Covenant and served His disciples, even washing their feet. Note that the hand of Jesus' betrayer was with Him on the table (Luke 22:21), but He still chose to eat the Passover meal with him. He confronted him without openly exposing him to the rest of the disciples, and at the same time extended grace and the New Covenant to him as well. He even washed His feet along with the rest of the disciples! This is not a theological treatise, but I can't help but wonder if the grace Jesus extended through this covenant meal might have been a last opportunity for Judas to repent of his sin and treachery.
>
> Jesus again puts emphasis on meals when He talks about eating and drinking at His table in His kingdom in the same verse

that He says to the disciples that they will sit on thrones judging the twelve Tribes of Israel! (Luke 22:30). Even the gathering in heaven is called, "The marriage supper of the Lamb" (Rev. 19:9). So it would seem that God puts a lot of stead in food, meals, and fellowship.

Interestingly in some covenant ceremonies following the feast, it is tradition to plant a tree. The necessity for covenant started with a tree and the fulfillment of covenant ended with a tree. And that tree, the cross, has become a symbol of remembrance for us. Let us never forget the cost of covenant, His life for ours. He is the covenant maker and He is the Covenant Keeper.

Chapter Three
Specific Covenants

Every covenant mentioned in the Bible builds on the previous one, giving us an ever-expanding picture and description of the Old Covenant until we have the fullness totally expressed in Jesus. Each covenant mentioned gives a deeper, richer image of Him, bursting with hope, joy, and expectancy, revealing a more intimate picture of our relationship with an extravagantly kind heavenly Father.

God initiated covenant. God confirmed covenant. God fulfilled covenant. And ultimately through Jesus as the Son of Man, He fulfilled both sides of the covenant because we could not measure up to our part of this eternal covenant. In every instance, God took the initiative. There was no agreement of equal parties. He initiated and cut covenant with His people, not vice versa. The heart of our Father and the heart of His covenant is, "You will be my people, and I will be your God" (Jeremiah 30:22).

Some of the more familiar covenants mentioned in the Bible are:

- Genesis 4: God's covenant with Adam and Eve in the garden when He covered them

- Genesis 6: God's covenant with Noah and the earth

- Genesis 15: God's covenant with Abraham, a generational promise to His offspring and to nations

- Exodus 19-20: God's covenant with Moses and the nation of Israel, and the giving of Torah

- II Samuel: God's covenant with David and the lineage of the Messiah to come
- Jesus, as He celebrated His last Passover, ushering in the new covenant

The Covenant from the Beginning

El Elyon actually cut the first covenant with creation before creation came to be. As He hovered over the void, the waters, the darkness, the chaos, He was seeing all of creation, the end from the beginning. At this point He must make eternal decisions to redeem His wonderful creation before it even began. Yeshua, Jesus, His only son, was crucified before the foundation of the world, which simply means *El Elyon* knew and made provision for us before He created us. Before there was a need He already was the answer.

As the Eternal hovered over this chaos, did He see you? Did He see me? Were we the joy that was set before him? In that moment just before He spoke and brought order out of the chaos, light out of darkness, He chose us. It was at this altar before creation of time that the Lord of all, the Eternal, cut covenant with His creation.

Our Creator, the master artist, began to release His covenant plan into creation incrementally with imagery, illustrations, examples, prophecies, and human events, all foreshadowing His son's birth, death, and resurrection. He wanted to imprint on our hearts and in our minds the depth of love and the true nature of the Father toward His beloved creation. As Creation unfolded with Adam and Eve, Noah, Abraham, Isaac, Jacob, Moses, and David, the Eternal took 4000 years to tell the full story of covenant.

The Covenant with Adam and Eve

In the garden following Adam and Eve's sin, the glory covering was gone and suddenly they knew they were naked. Shame entered into the earth. Ashamed and exposed, they reached for a fig leaf to hide. This was the first religious act of man: to do something to try to fix themselves. It didn't work for them then and it does not work for us now.

Jesus had already made the supreme sacrifice, but now it became necessary for His sacrifice to be walked out in the earth realm. The Eternal sacrificed an animal, possibly a lamb or ram, shed its blood, and covered them with the skin, the first picture of covenant. This became the perpetual image of what would be required of Jesus: the blood of the Lamb to take away our sin and to cover us. In the book of Hebrews we read, "without the shedding of blood there is no remission of sin." Adam and Eve were covered by the blood sacrifice.

The Covenant with Noah

"But Noah found grace in the eyes of the Lord. And God said unto Noah, The end of all flesh is come before me; for the earth is filled with violence through them; and, behold, I will destroy them with the earth. Make thee an ark of gopher wood; And God spake unto Noah, saying, Go forth of the ark, thou, and thy wife, and thy sons, and thy sons' wives with thee. Bring forth with thee every living thing that is with thee,…the LORD said in His heart, I will not again curse the ground any more for man's sake; for the imagination of man's heart is evil from his youth; neither will I again smite any more every thing living, as I have done. While the earth remaineth, seedtime and harvest, and cold and heat, and summer and winter, and day and night shall not cease. And I, behold, I establish my covenant with you, and with your seed after you; And with every living creature that is with you, And I will establish my covenant with you; neither shall all flesh   be cut off any more by the waters of a flood; neither shall there any more be a flood to destroy the

earth. And God said, This is the token of the covenant which I make between me and you and every living creature that is with you, for perpetual generations: I do set my bow in the cloud, and it shall be for a token of a covenant between me and the earth. And it shall come to pass, when I bring a cloud over the earth, that the bow shall be seen in the cloud: And I will remember my covenant, which is between me and you."
(Gen 6:8,13,14; 8:16-17, 21-22; 9:9-15 KJV)

After the garden the next picture of covenant is with Noah. Noah's name means a quiet, resting place, a place to dwell, and to give comfort. Isn't that a wonderful name? The Lord was wooing His bride, offering her comfort, a resting place, a place to dwell with Him. "Dwell" and "habitation" are covenant words, opening our eyes to see not only His goodness and gentleness, but also His commitment to marry us and dwell together with us intimately and eternally.

The rainbow as seen from above the earth is complete circle, a multi-colored wedding band of light. Several years ago I was asleep on a plane coming home from Rome when my friend, Bunny Warlen, abruptly woke me up saying "Look! Look!" I looked out my window and there below us was a rainbow, a complete circle. It was an amazing sight and confirmed to me what I had read about in science. A full, complete dazzling circle of light. As our *Go'el*, our Kinsman Redeemer, comes to redeem and marry us, this is the wedding band He offers us: a brilliant, multi-colored circle of light.

There are seven distinct colors of a rainbow, each with a precise meaning. Remember the oath of covenant means to *seven* someone and also means completion and fullness. Through this rainbow, God is speaking covenant seven times with the seven colors, seven distinct circles.

The Bible tells us in Ezekiel and in Revelation that there is a rainbow around His throne.

"And above the firmament over their heads was the likeness of a throne, in appearance like a sapphire stone ... Like the appearance of a rainbow in a cloud on a rainy day, so was the appearance of the brightness all around it. This was the appearance of the likeness of the glory of the Lord" (Eze. 1:27-28)

"Behold, a throne set in heaven, and One sat on the throne. And He who sat there was like a jasper and a sardius stone in appearance; and there was a rainbow around the throne, in appearance like an emerald" (Rev. 4:1-3)

Each time Jesus looks at us from His throne, He sees us through our wedding band of light, through the seven colors of covenant as His beloved bride, redeemed, pure, holy. Complete without spot or blemish. He sees us in the fullness of what we will be at the marriage supper of the Lamb spoken of in Revelation.

The Covenant of Abraham

Earlier we discussed the framework and the specifics of making a covenant. All of these tenets were present in Jehovah's covenant with Abram who became Abraham. When Jehovah called for Abram to make a covenant with Him, Abram was already familiar with covenants and the elements required. But this covenant would be cut with a holy God, quite different from man to man covenants. How was this covenant actually worked out in the everyday world of Abraham?

A covenant causes movement, a change of identity, and releases blessing and inheritance. God met with Abraham several times to establish covenant, each time going a little deeper and increasing Abraham's wealth, provision, family, and possessions. The Lord knew Abraham, but it took almost twenty years of walking in favor with God for Abraham to begin to know and trust Jehovah *Elohim* enough to agree to cut covenant with Him. Remember there is always a choice with covenant.

Genesis 12 begins with Jehovah calling Abram out of Ur into a new land and promising him blessings. He was given land in

Canaan and there Abram built an altar and worshipped this God who was speaking to him. As we contemplate the early portion of Abram's life, we do not find a lot of history prior to this call. How did Abram recognize Jehovah's voice? Had he heard the story of Noah? The Bible tells us that the eyes of the Lord are moving over the earth looking for men whose hearts are turned toward Him. Was Abram's heart already turned toward the God of Noah? All we do know for sure is that God chose Abram, Abram obeyed, and the first action he took was to worship. He built an altar, sacrificed an animal, and worshiped Jehovah. That should say something to all of us. I believe the foundation of our lives as we walk out our covenant in the earth with our God, should always be the same: obedience and worship.

As Abram obeyed and worshiped, Jehovah-God blessed him. He went into Egypt as a lowly shepherd and came out a wealthy man, favored by God. Interestingly, others saw the favor of God upon him and the kings of the region aligned with him. This was repeated on a far greater scale when Abram's grandson, Jacob and his sons went into Egypt as poor shepherds and four hundred years later came out with the riches of Egypt and the magnified favor of God upon them.

As Jehovah was teaching Abram to trust Him and to learn His character, He was also yearning for something from Abram. He longed for relationship. God wanted to establish His own name in the earth and He chose Abram. Little by little, as God made and kept His promises to Abram, Abram began to change from the fearful shepherd who would lie about his wife's identity to protect himself, into a strong warrior who would face a formidable enemy to rescue his nephew Lot. What made the difference? Covenant. Abram began to believe and trust Jehovah-God to do what He said He would do and Jehovah gave him favor, possessions, and protection.

Then came the day, recorded in Genesis 15-17, when Jehovah *Elohim* actually cut covenant with Abram. Everything changed. Abram's relationship with God shifted to a new level. Abram's identity and name changed as did Sarai's. Abram, which means father became Abraham, the father of many nations and Sarai became Sarah, a noble lady or queen. Abraham, the father of nations, was also known as God's Chosen.

They came into increased inheritance in the land and the boundaries of Abram's land were set. God's promises were activated in the earth in a new way and Abram's descendants would be forever known as The Chosen of God.

The most amazing thing to me is Jehovah Himself, who had said to Abraham, "You will know me by my name" took Abraham's name and is still known today as the God of Abraham, Isaac, and Jacob. Now Abraham and God had the same name. Abraham's enemies became God's enemies and Abraham's friends became God's friends. At this point, God deeded the land, today known as Israel, to Abraham and his descendants. Abraham was known as a friend of God and he walked in great favor the rest of his days in the earth.

Friends and covenant partners share meals together. Abraham and God shared a meal at Mamre. When the three strangers showed up expectedly, Abraham recognized his friend immediately. And just as friends and covenant partners do, they ate together and discussed heart issues. God had heard the cries from the cities of Sodom and Gomorrah, and with a heavy heart, He discussed His plans with Abraham. Abraham was so secure in his relationship with Jehovah, with boldness he bargained for the life of his nephew. Face-to-face, secure relationship. Covenant.

Abraham's covenant cut was circumcision. Now his seed would pass through the cut of covenant. Abraham's heart's desire, a son Isaac, was born after Abraham was circumcised and was the first son of this generational covenant. Even today Abraham's descendants, the Jewish people walk in great favor, especially in the economic realm. As Abraham's covenant partner, Jehovah provided for Abraham, avenged him, fought for him, and gave him inheritance. And they each carried the other's name.

Later, when he climbed Mount Moriah with his son Isaac, Abraham went to worship with a knife in his hand. Here the Lord would reveal yet another covenant name to him: *Jehovah Jirah*. This is the only time this covenant name appears. "The Lord will provide." The covenant name Jehovah *Rohe*, our shepherd is the provider of our physical needs. The name *Jirah* is related only to His provision of the ram in the bush, the blood sacrifice. "The Lord will provide Himself, the lamb." (Genesis 22:8, KJV) *Jirah* means to appear, be present, to see, and to provide. The ram in the bush was provided as the blood sacrifice for Abraham and for Isaac.

If you want generational blessing to be released to your children, follow Abraham's example, obey and worship through covenant. Walk with Jehovah *jirah,* the God who truly did provide Himself as the lamb, the sacrifice for our sin.

The Covenant at Mt. Sinai

When Moses came down from Mt. Sinai, he brought the Torah. Note that even this word ends with *ah*, the breath sound of the name of Jehovah. As a Gentile watching Charlton Heston play Moses on the big screen, my understanding was that there were just the two tablets with the Ten Commandments written on them. In actuality, as Moses spent forty days on the mountain with Jehovah, he received the entire Law with specific instructions on how to live, how to eat, how to worship, how to make the priestly clothes, how to set up the tabernacle, and so much more. Every aspect of their daily lives was laid out in intricate detail for a healthy, godly, and morally pure lifestyle.

These details outline the conditions and regulations of covenant just as required by the covenant ceremonies mentioned earlier. Torah is the document or testimony of covenant for the Tribes of Israel. The giving and receiving of Torah is celebrated at the Feast of *Shavuot* or Pentecost and traditional Orthodox refer to that feast as the day Jehovah betroth the nation of Israel.

Specific Covenants

The Torah contains the preamble, the name of *Elohim* as the God of witness, the prologue describing the intended relationship and responsibilities of both parties, the blessings and curses of obedience or disobedience, the generational succession arrangement, and the yearly plan of remembrance with the celebration of the feasts.

"Torah is not a job description, it is a doctor's prescription for a healthy life, full of joy and happiness." Says my friend, Stephen Johnson. Deuteronomy 4 records the charge given by Moses to the new generation getting ready to go into the promised land with Joshua. It is clear God's intention for the nation of Israel was to be a great, mighty nation in the earth, full of justice, wisdom, and understanding. These attributes, which reflect His very own nature, would draw other nations to seek and know Him. But like we all do sometimes, the people regarded the Torah as a set of do's and do not's, a job description. This mindset brings us into the bondage of legalism and death.

> "I'm teaching you the rules and regulations that God commanded me, so that you may live by them in the land you are entering to take up ownership. Keep them. Practice them. You'll become wise and understanding. When people hear and see what's going on, they'll say, "What a great nation! So wise, so understanding! We've never seen anything like it." Yes. What other great nation has gods that are intimate with them the way God, our God, is with us, always ready to listen to us? And what other great nation has rules and regulations as good and fair as this revelation that I'm setting before you today. Know this well, then take it to heart right now: God is in heaven above; God is on earth below. He's the only God there is. Obediently live by His rules and commands which I'm giving you today so that you'll live well and your children after you. Oh you'll live a long time in the land that God, your God is giving you." (Deuteronomy 4:5-8, 39-40, MSG)

The Torah was also given to show us the holy standard required by Jehovah *Elohim* to walk the blood path of covenant without death coming immediately. No one could keep it. These Books of the Law were given to demonstrate what would be required to enter back into the relationship God had with Adam before the fall. It was the standard we could never reach, regardless of how hard we tried. The Torah was given so we would realize how much we needed a *go'el*, a kinsman redeemer, to marry us as a widow because our earthly bodies would have to die because of sin.

Adam brought death into the earth in the garden and had to leave the holy presence of God. Death had come to steal our inheritance as a son and a bride. Death had come to the house of creation. Now all of creation, which includes us, was a widow. We needed a kinsman redeemer to marry and redeem us. We needed Him to defeat our enemy Death and set us free from bondage. We needed full restoration of the inheritance we lost in the garden. We needed the Torah to show us it was impossible without a *go'el*, a redeemer.

The kinsman redeemer is first mentioned in the book of Exodus of the Torah. When God declared the "I Will's" repeated in the Passover Feast, He was referring to the responsibilities of a kinsman redeemer, a *go'el*.

> "And I have also heard the groaning of the children of Israel whom the Egyptians keep in bondage, and I have remembered my covenant. Therefore say to the children of Israel: "I am the Lord; I will bring you out from under the burdens of the Egyptians, I will rescue you from their bondage, and I will redeem (*go'el*, H1350, Strongs) you with an outstretched arm and with great judgements. I will take you as my people and I will be your God. Then you shall know that I am the Lord your God who brings you out from under the burdens of the Egyptians. And I will bring you into the land which I swore to give to Abraham, Isaac and Jacob; and I will give it to you as a heritage; I am the Lord." (Exodus 6:5-9)

Here the Lord says first, "I have remembered my covenant." When He remembered the children of Israel in Egypt, it was the fullness of time for them, and He brought them out of captivity. As the *Go'el* Redeemer, Jehovah stated His vows of covenant with His people:

- I will bring you out from the burdens you are under (Pay your debts)
- I will rescue you from bondage (Buy you back from slavery)
- I will redeem you (Marry you as though you were a widow)
- I will bring you out with great judgments (Will avenge you)
- You will know me. Note: "know" here means to have intimate knowledge and understanding of a person as when Abraham *knew* Sarah and she became pregnant.

Upon receiving this document, the Torah, Moses read it aloud to the Israelites in the desert. They acknowledged and accepted the terms of the covenant. Following Aaron's installment as High Priest, they sealed their acceptance with blood sacrifice. Were they aware as they made the oath of covenant, "All you have said, we will do," that they were stepping into an agreement with *Elohim* that would have required their death unless He had provided the blood sacrifice of the lamb? I believe that to the best of their ability, they meant to keep all of the words of this covenant. But like all of us, they still had the original sin nature from Adam and regardless of how sincere they were or how hard they tried, they could not keep this law. Again, looking forward in time, their Messiah, *Elohim* Himself, would come to pay the price for their disobedience.

The Covenant of David and Jonathan

I love to look at the covenant between Jonathan and David. Jonathan was a prince, the son of the king. What a wonderful picture of our relationship with the Prince of Peace, Jesus, the Son of the King of the universe.

Jonathan and David came from separate worlds, one a prince from the royal family and the other a shepherd from the hills of Judea. Because of God's favor on him, Jonathan honored and respected David, even loving him as a brother. As mentioned earlier, it was not an uncommon thing in this culture to make covenants with other men. It was a lifelong vow to walk together as brothers in the earth, as in "I've got your back" brothers. Even after Jonathan's death, David honored this covenant when he invited Mephibosheth, Jonathan's lame son, to sit at his table as one of his own sons.

I believe the Lord highlighted their relationship as yet another picture of the blessing of covenant relationship with the Prince of Peace, Jesus.

> "Now when he had finished speaking to Saul, the soul of Jonathan was knit to the soul of David, and Jonathan loved him as his own soul. Saul took him that day, and would not let him go home to his father's house anymore. Then Jonathan and David made a covenant, because he loved him as his own soul. And Jonathan took off the robe that was on him and gave it to David, with his armor, even to his sword and his bow and his belt." (I Samuel 18:1-4).

The first detail we note here is that they loved each other and were united in soul and spirit. Then the outward working of the covenant came. A covenant is always about relationship and they each had a choice to enter into covenant or not. They both chose to do so. A covenant is always a choice.

First they exchanged coats or robes. This made a difference in David's daily life. During this era there was no social media to let everyone know which people were the VIPs and who were the ordinary folks. How would you recognize a king or prince? Their clothes told the story. When David put on Jonathan's robe, everyone recognized him as a prince. This robe carried authority. Only a prince wore this type of robe and received honor and respect as a future leader in the tribe or nation. Wherever David went wearing Jonathan's robe, he had the authority and the identity of a prince.

But what about Jonathan? Was he willing to wear the rough, dirty robe of a shepherd and be recognized as such? We are not told this, but our covenant partner Jesus did just that. Our Prince of Peace was clothed in splendor and holiness. He sat on a throne of glory with myriads of angelic worshipers crying, "Holy! Holy! Holy!" He was honored with the highest acclaim. In the Psalms we read "He wraps Himself in light and rides on the wings of the wind." But He was willing to take off all of His splendor, His glory, and take on our robe of humanity.

"Although from the beginning He had the nature of God He did not reckon His equality with God a treasure to be tightly grasped. Nay, He stripped Himself of His glory, and took on Him the nature of a bondservant by becoming a man like other men. And being recognized as truly human, He humbled Himself and even stooped to die; yes, to die on a cross" (Phil. 2:6-8, MSG).

Our Prince put on our filthy covering of self-righteousness, our sin, and gave us beauty for ashes, the oil of joy for mourning, and a garment of praise for the spirit of heaviness as noted in Isaiah.

He became the Son of Man that we could become sons of God. Clothed in His righteousness and His love, we reflect His glory to a dark and wounded world. According to Jesus, here is what our covenant robe should look like:

"Are you tired? Worn out? Burned out on religion? Come to me. Get away with me and you'll recover your life. I'll show you how to take a real rest. Walk with me and work with me—watch how I do it. Learn the unforced rhythms of grace. I won't lay anything heavy or ill-fitting on you. Keep company with me and you'll learn to live freely and lightly" (Matthew 11:29-30, MSG).

As we are clothed in our covenant robe of light we reflect His light and His love to the world around us. We learn the unforced rhythms of His grace. We learn and walk in His freedom.

Jonathan and David exchanged weapons, which meant "your enemies are now my enemies." Why do you think our enemy, Satan, hates us so much? His chief aim is to destroy Jesus, his enemy from before the world was formed. He failed and was thrown from heaven, but he continues to try to get the Son's glory. He knows the best way to wound Jesus' heart is to destroy the love of His life, His bride, His covenant partner.

Now we can see why we need Jesus' own weapons, the spiritual armor from Ephesians, so much because His weapons are mighty to the pulling down of strongholds and defeating the enemy of our souls. First and foremost we must cover our heads with His salvation. His righteousness becomes our breastplate, His truth our belt of strength. His peace is released as we walk in this earth. Knowing and hiding His word in our heart, we go forth praying always in the spirit. It is imperative that we call on our covenant partner who is also a mighty warrior. As our *Go'el* He protects and avenges us. He is Lord *Sabaoth*, the commander of the angel armies. We must suit up with His armor and be ready to go to war alongside of Him.

Psalm 45 paints an awesome picture for us. As the King, the commander of the angel armies rides forth on a white horse in full battle array, coming to claim His bride, His covenant scars are always visible to His enemy. And His enemy cannot touch His bride because she is protected by the power of the blood of her Kinsman Redeemer, her Blood Avenger, her covenant partner.

The Covering, The *Tallit*

"God spoke to Moses: Speak to the people of Israel. Tell them that from now on they are to make tassels on the corners of their garments and to mark each corner tassel with a blue thread. When you look at the tassels you'll remember and keep all the commandments of God, and not get distracted by everything you feel or see that seduces you into infidelities. The tassels will signal remembrance and observance of all my commandments, to live a holy life to God. I am your God who rescued you from the land of Egypt to be your personal God. Yes, I am God, Your God." (Numbers 15:37-41, MSG)

Just as Jesus' covenant sign, His scars, are visible to our enemy, Jehovah desired a covenant sign to be visible in the earth for His people. He chose the *tzitzit* and the *tallit* which comes from a word meaning cover.

Both in Numbers 15:38 and Deuteronomy 22:12 God commanded each head of household to cover themselves with a four-cornered garment with fringe on each corner. This is known today as a *tallit* or prayer shawl. The fringe, called the *tzitzit*, is the outward sign of covenant to be worn by all generations. Each fringe is knotted with five distinct knots and has a blue thread woven into it. Two fringes represented the Law, the Ten Commandments.

Covering has always been strategic and important to the Lord. Throughout the Bible, we see the covering of the blood of Jesus pictured in numerous ways.

- In heaven His throne, the mercy seat, is always covered by worship.
- In the earth, the mercy seat of the tabernacle was covered by golden cherubim and a veil.
- Once a year, the mercy seat was covered with the blood of a lamb.
- In the garden, Adam and Eve were covered with His glory, but they lost this glory because of their sin. *Elohim* killed an animal, shedding its blood, and covered them with the skin of the sacrificed animal.

- He covered the earth with clouds and the rainbow of light, releasing the light of His glory with the covenant circle of seven colors, "*sevening*" Himself to creation.
- As He cut a covenant with Abram, He covered him with a deep sleep to protect him from the holiness of His presence as He, personally, came to cut covenant.
- In the wilderness, He covered the tabernacle with the cloud by day and the fire by night.
- He covered the top of Mount Sinai with clouds and fire.
- He covered Moses in the cleft of the rock as He passed by.

After coming out of Egypt, Jehovah desired face to face relationship with His children. Because they were afraid of the cloud filled with lightning and thunder, Moses went up to represent them. God appointed Aaron as high priest to go into the Tabernacle to represent the people, presenting the daily blood sacrifice. Jehovah then covered this Holy tent with His glory, the cloud by day and the fire by night.

But Jehovah still longed to meet with His people individually. There was not enough room for the thousands of fathers to meet with the Lord in that one small tent in the desert. Jehovah made a way; covenant made it possible.

Following the seven days of dedication of Aaron and his sons as priests before the Lord, Jehovah instructed them to sacrifice a lamb two times a day, morning and evening. It was at these times the people were called to meet with Jehovah.

> "For generations to come this will be the daily burnt offering made in the LORD's presence at the entrance to the tent of meeting. There I will meet with you to speak to you. I will also meet with the Israelites there, and my glory will make this place holy." (Ex. 29:42-43 GW)

An interesting side note here: When in Israel we visited Shilo, the place where the Tabernacle stood for 369 years. The guide stated:

Specific Covenants

"Note the Tabernacle stood in what appears to be a bowl, surrounded by mountains. As soon as the people came over the mountain and could see the Tabernacle, they were considered to be standing on Holy Ground." As I read this passage from Exodus I am reminded that if they could see the Tabernacle, they were considered to be in His Holy presence.

The *tallit* represented the covering and the *tzitzit* or fringe was an outward sign of covenant. Every morning during the morning sacrifice the father slipped out of his own tent to face the Holy Tabernacle wearing his *tallit*, the sign he was covered by the blood of covenant. It must have been a joy to Abba Father's heart as He listened to the fathers recite the *Shema* in the hearing of their own children:

"Hear, O Israel. The Lord thy God is one. You shall worship the Lord thy God with all of your heart, with all of your soul, with all of your mind, with all of your strength..." (Deut. 6:4-9, Deut. 11:13-21).

In the Jewish culture, a thread bare, worn *tallit* is an item of honor. It speaks of the dedicated prayer life of its owner and is treated with respect and reverence. Usually a young man is given his *tallit* at his *Bar Mitzvah*. It is sometimes used as the *chuppah*/canopy at his wedding and it could possibly be the only one he would have all of his life. At his burial one of the *tzitzit* is cut off, signifying that he is no longer under the law he has lived by in this world. It is then wrapped around his head and can be referred to as a napkin. When Lazarus was raised from the dead, Jesus told them to "remove the napkin from around his head." When not being worn, the *tallit* is carefully folded and kept in a designated place so that it is protected from casual disregard. Many times it is customary for an individual to fold his *tallit* in his own personal way. This would become an important sign to Jesus' followers after His resurrection.

The *tzitzit* is still worn by observant Jewish men and even some women today. Recently I attended a predominantly Jewish gathering in Washington, D.C. During one of the meetings I found myself sitting by a very gregarious Jewish rabbi. He was quite open and, as always, I had many questions about Jewish traditions. I mentioned the prayer shawl and, jovial man that he was, he chuckled and pulled open his coat, pointing to the fringe he was wearing on his shirttail. We laughed together and became friends.

Not long after, I was walking down an avenue in Disney World and I noticed two couples in front of us, both Jewish. The young men were wearing tee shirts, Levis and tennis shoes. What set them apart was the small *kippahs* on their heads and the long fringe hanging from their belts. What a blending of the old and the new, still remembering this generational covenant of 4000 years.

Sometimes in churches today we see men and women wearing a *tallit*. Could this be a beautiful and symbolic sign that the Lord is restoring the church to the Jewish roots of our faith? Just a small understanding of the *tallit*, Sabbath, and the feasts has enriched my relationship with the Lord and deepened my revelation of our New Covenant. He really is the same yesterday, today, and forever. He never changes and His covenant is eternal.

Translated in the Bible as wings, hem, skirt or cover, the four-cornered garment with the *tzitzit* is found in so many references. When we talk about being under His wings, carried on eagles' wings or take refuge under His wings, we are speaking covenant language referring to the *tallit*, bringing to remembrance our *Go'el*, our Kinsman Redeemer.

When David cut off the hem of Saul's garment, he was cutting off his fringe, his *tzitzit*. Afterward David was very grieved. This covenant was between Saul and God; David did not have the authority to touch such a holy thing.

In the story of Ruth and Boaz she said, "I am Ruth, your maidservant. Take your maidservant under your wing, for you are a close relative" (Ruth 3:9). The Hebrew word here for close relative is *go'el,* a kinsman redeemer. The Hebrew marriage is official when the bride comes under her groom's covering or *tallit*. Boaz brought this

Gentile Moabite woman into the covenant of Abraham by covering her with his skirt or *tallit*. She asked for and received redemption under the covenant of the kinsman redeemer, the *go'el*. As an honorable man, Boaz covered her with his prayer shawl so that if anyone saw her they knew immediately he was bringing her into covenant with himself.

The Lord used the same word again in Ezekiel 16:8 when He spoke to Jerusalem "I spread my wing over thee, and covered thy nakedness."

The Messianic prophetic Scripture from Malachi 4:2, "So shall the sun of righteousness arise with healing in His wings," is a very powerful Scripture concerning the healing ministry of Jesus, who wore the *tzitzit* on the hem of His garment. Remember the woman who touched Jesus' hem and was healed? She knew about this Messianic prophecy. By touching the *tzitzit* of His prayer shawl she was affirming her belief that truly Jesus was her Messiah. She understood the power and authority of the wings of the Messiah, so she knew she could find healing there. There are numerous other accounts of people touching His *tzitzit* to receive their healing because they understood covenant.

Read Psalm 91 with the new eyes of covenant:

> "He who dwells in the secret place of the Most High shall abide under the shadow (*covering of covenant*) of the Almighty. I will say of the Lord, "He is my refuge and my fortress; my God, in Him I will trust.
>
> "Surely He shall deliver you from the snare of the fowler and from the perilous pestilence. He shall cover you with His feathers, and under His wings (*covering of covenant*) you shall take refuge." (Psalm 91:1-2)

God spent four thousand years meticulously preparing for the new to come. He desired a culture of people in the earth and He started with covenant. Our *Go'el* is the same yesterday, today, and forever. Come under His wings for healing, restoration, and redemption. He is our Covenant Keeper. He is our *go'el*.

Chapter Four
The Law of the Kinsman Redeemer, the Go'el

In the beginning our Father set laws, guidelines, and choices within the Law of Redemption so we could more clearly see His Son and His redemptive purposes. According to the Law of Redemption found in the Torah, the nearest male blood relative had the duty of preserving the family name and property, entailing several aspects.

Adam had no brother when he brought death into creation. Adam was fashioned from clay and the Holy Spirit breathed life into his body. From one man came all of the people of the earth. But Adam made a wrong choice and brought sin and death into the earth. Creation, including all mankind, became a widow. Jesus became flesh as Adam's brother to qualify as the near kinsman to buy back and redeem the widow of creation. The book of Revelation says in chapter five, "Who is worthy to open the scrolls? No one was found worthy. Except one, the Lamb, Yeshua Jesus.

Being a near kinsman was only one of the three requirements of a *go'el*. He must also possess the means by which to redeem the widow; the redemption had to be strictly voluntary. He had the free will to choose to buy back the inheritance and marry the widow of the dead, or he could walk away. It was always his choice. Jesus met all three of these requirements according to the covenant. There are many other Messianic prophecies which were necessary to be fulfilled, but we will only focus on those directly related to His being our Kinsman Redeemer.

Jesus was Jewish. In the patriarchal society of early Israel, lineage was traced through the father or male line. In order to qualify as our *Go'el*, redeeming all of creation, He had to be a descendant of Abraham, Isaac, and Jacob, of the Tribe of Judah, in the line of King David. His mother Mary was also from the Tribe of Judah.

As a kinsman redeemer He must possess the ability to pay the price required to buy her back. Although there were many generations prior to the giving of the Torah, the requirements were set in motion in the Garden of Eden when death came into the earthly realm. Did Jesus have access to the riches and wealth to buy back all of humanity? And what was the high cost of this payment?

> "Knowing that you were not redeemed with corruptible things, like silver or gold, from your aimless conduct received by tradition from your fathers, but with the precious blood of Christ, as of a lamb without blemish and without spot. He indeed was foreordained before the foundation of the world, but was manifest in these last times for you who through Him believe in God, who raised Him from the dead and gave Him glory, so that your faith and hope are in God." (1 Peter 1:18-21)

He could only pay this high cost if He was the Son of God, born of a virgin. Medically we know that the mother's blood never mixes with the baby's blood while the baby is in the womb. Jesus, as our Kinsman Redeemer was the Son of God and His blood was pure, holy, and sanctified, fully capable of paying the debt required by the covenant with Abraham. Remember, only God walked between the pieces of the sacrifice in His covenant with Abraham. He knew Abraham could never pay the price required. Yes, the covenant was made with Abraham and his seed, but this covenant was the next step of bringing the Kinsman Redeemer into creation through the seed of Abraham for redemption of His bride. God, in His mercy was preparing the way for His only Son to become our Kinsman Redeemer, our *Go'el*.

As the last qualification the kinsman redeemer had to be totally willing to redeem the widow. Free to choose or decline-the choice was his. Jesus made it clear to His followers that He would make the right choice when the time came.

> "I am the good shepherd; and I know My sheep, and am known by My own. As the Father knows Me, even so I know the Father; and I lay down My life for the sheep ... Therefore My Father loves Me, because I lay down My life that I may take it again. No one takes it from Me, but I lay it down of Myself. I have power to lay it down, and I have power to take it again. This command I have received from My Father." (John 10:14-18)

When Jesus prayed in the garden of Gethsemane He said, "Father, if it is Your will, take this cup away from Me; nevertheless, not My will, but Yours, be done" (Luke 22:42).

He had met all of the requirements to be our *Go'el*, our Kinsman Redeemer. In this moment of grief and decision, He looked beyond the pain and suffering that was to come. He saw His bride.

As a bride we had sold ourselves into slavery by our sin. We had looked to others for support and provision. We had chosen to drink from stagnant cisterns rather than cry out for the living water. Although we were wrapped in our filthy rags, destitute, and hopeless, He had compassion on us. He could see past this pitiful picture of a widow and knew He could cleanse us from all unrighteousness and make us a pure and spotless bride by the purity of His own blood. He looked past the cross and saw the wedding feast. He said yes. He chose us.

The Four Actions of a Kinsman Redeemer

Qualifying was just the first step. Not only did he have to be a near kinsman, have the resources and be fully willing to do so, he had to actively begin to move forward on behalf of the widow. There were four specific actions he would need to take to fulfill this role. He must marry the widow, become her avenger, buy her back out of slavery by paying her debts, and restore her inheritance which had been lost. The land of Israel was allotted to specific tribes, and could not be permanently sold. All of the land returned to the original families in the year of Jubilee, a 50-year cycle. Therefore should a male die prematurely with no heirs, the first child of a *go'el* marriage would actually be the heir to the dead man's property lest his name not be remembered in the nation.

Marry the Widow

> "If brothers dwell together, and one of them dies and has no son, the widow of the dead man shall not be married to a stranger outside the family; her husband's brother shall go in to her, take her as his wife, and perform the duty of a husband's brother to her. And it shall be that the firstborn son which she bears will succeed to the name of his dead brother, that his name may not be blotted out of Israel."
> (Deut. 25:5-6)

When there was death in the house it was a tradition to tear the clothing and put ashes on the heads of the family members. In the garden when Adam brought death to the human race through his sin, we essentially became widows, because there was death in the house of Adam. In fact all of creation became a widow. From that moment we were covered in ashes.

But Jesus, our Kinsman Redeemer, came to restore the inheritance we lost in the garden through Adam's sin. He came to wash away the ashes of death and give us beauty again. He came to exchange our black, torn clothing of widowhood for the purity of a spotless bridal gown.

I want to address these bitter ashes. Ashes signify loss. Sometimes these ashes can be a good reminder of a sacrifice we willingly laid on the altar of the Lord. He took it and we no longer have to deal with the consequences of that issue. Those would be good ashes.

But when loss comes in our lives, whether spiritual, emotional, or physical, it may feel as though we have received bitter ashes. Perhaps something precious has been taken or stolen; a relationship you once held dear is gone; expectations were not met; dreams were dashed to the ground, leaving you with an empty heart and bitter ashes.

Or it is possible there has been the loss of a spouse or a child.

Very bitter ashes.

Remember covenant is an exchange. Isaiah 61 promises beauty for your ashes. He will give you joy for your empty heart. You will wear a glorious garment of praise instead of being weighed down by the heaviness of your widow's torn, black mourning clothes. These verses too remind us of what our Go'el came to do for us.

I love to hear testimonies of believers because no matter how bad things get, they always come to the part of the story when they say, "But God…"

But God! Simple words that change everything.

Is your world going to hell in a hand basket? But God!

Have you lost it all, bankrupt spiritually or physically? But God!

Are you or someone you love caught in addictions or diagnosed with cancer? But God!

These are hard and difficult places to be. It would be great if life were a Hallmark movie where it always works out beautifully at the end. As mature Christians we know there is hard stuff out there and it doesn't always work out the way we would have liked.

On those days that seem so dreary, when your hope is deferred and you are emotionally spent, all you can do is cry out to your *Go'el* for deliverance and remember covenant. And as He promised, He comes. Our bridegroom comes. Our circumstances may not change, but because He is faithful to His covenant, He comes. He may not still the storm, but He stills His child in the storm. He keeps His covenant to never leave us nor forsake us. He comes. "But God!"

The day I sat in the bathroom floor with my sister, Fran, as she wailed in bitter anguish, I experienced what bitter ashes looked like. Her seventeen-year-old son had died suddenly. The harshness of her pain burned to the depth of my soul. I had no answers. All I could do was hold her and say, "I love you." I remember asking my nephew, Eddy, a pastor, "Where is the grace?" because the agony was so raw and deep that breathing was an effort. In his quiet, reassuring voice he answered, "Well, I guess the fact that we are here at the funeral home, walking through this together is grace."

I've heard Ray Hughes say, "You can make it through hell if you don't stop walking." It felt like we were in hell during that season but we all, especially my sister and her family, simply had to keep walking. It took years for her to come out of those ashes. Yet there came the day, as she gazed upon the precious face of her first granddaughter, she was able to embrace the goodness of life once again. The beauty came in the innocence of a baby. But God!

Are there still ashes in her life? Sure. In mine? Yes. We all have questions about our ashes. Yet each time we kneel at the table of communion, we remember His promise of exchange, of covenant. As we bring our heartache, our ashes and lay them in His nail-pierced hands we trust His promise of exchange. Remember, not only did David receive Jonathan's robe, Jonathan took David's ragged shepherd's coat. The exchange of covenant.

Several years back I was taking communion in my living room by myself. That day I knelt down at my coffee table, prayed, and broke a piece of bread asking for His peace and joy, thanking Him for His sacrifice. I drank the wine, again thanking Him for the blood that cleanses me and takes away my sin. Then I stood up to leave. Suddenly it seemed as if He shouted, "Wait a minute!" I quickly fell back to my knees, my heart beating rapidly and my ears ready to hear. Then the Lord spoke something that changed forever how I would receive His body and blood at the communion table.

"You came to this table to receive and so did I. Covenant means exchange. I brought you peace, joy, healing, and forgiveness. But you brought me nothing." I was shocked. What did I have to bring to the King? He continued, "I want that fear I see lurking inside of your heart. And I want that attitude you have when you hear a certain sister's name being called. If I give you my royal robes, I expect for you to give me your ashes and that dirty, ragged garment in exchange. Covenant means exchange. Both ways."

I wasn't sure how to respond. Yes, I was aware of the fear and the attitude, but I thought I needed to wrestle a little, work it out and then repent. That day He simply said, "Stop the wrestling and just hand it over." That seemed too easy, but what choice did I have. I physically used my hand to place the fear and attitude into His open hand. Then He said, "You can go now."

It was over. I was stunned. I went about my day and pondered what had happened.

Over the next few weeks others began to notice some changes in me of which I was unaware. My dentist, Jeff, said, "I've worked in your mouth for years, and I've never seen you not tense up when I turned on the drill. What's happened to you." Oh! That fear was gone.

I drove our car across the Mississippi River bridge and realized on the other side that I hadn't had to grip the wheel tightly, tense up and pray all the way across. The fear of high bridges was gone.

Other little areas which normally would have caused me to feel anxious were just gone. Jesus did it! He literally took all those little niggling fears away. I didn't have to wrestle before I went to the dentist or drive across a high bridge any more. And the attitude? The next time I saw this gal, I was genuinely happy to see her. I gave her a hug and we had a wonderful conversation about our children and grandchildren. The attitude was gone. Exchange! Covenant really is exchange.

We cannot receive His beauty and His peace unless we are willing to give Him our ashes, our sorrow, our burden. We exchange our ashes for His kindness, His grace, His mercy. We exchange our heartache for a spirit of gratitude and worship. We then trust His promise as our Kinsman Redeemer that He will make the total exchange of our death for His life.

Our *Go'el*, whose name is Faithful and True, gives us a beautiful garment of praise for our torn widow's garment smeared with ashes. As we step under His covenant wings, His *tallit*, we have assurance that this Son of righteousness has truly risen with healing in His wings to shift us from our widowhood to be His bride.

Become the Blood Avenger

"The avenger of blood himself shall put the murderer to death; when He meets him, He shall put him to death" (Numbers 35:19-20).

Our Kinsman Redeemer brings us justice.

The Hebrew word *go'el* is from the verb, *ga'al*, which here means to be near of kin or to redeem the nearest relative of a murdered person. God designated cities of refuge for the purpose of protecting innocent people against being punished for crimes that they either did not commit or committed accidentally. It was the right and duty of the near kinsman to slay the murderer if he found him outside a City of Refuge. The case had to be investigated by the authorities of the city, and the willful murderer was not to be spared. He was regarded as an impure, polluted person and delivered up to the *go'el*. If the offense was accidental manslaughter, then the fugitive must remain within the City of Refuge until the death of the high priest.

In our democratic society we go by a different set of laws for murder, theft, and other crimes against people. The state carries out the sentence. But under the Law of the *Go'el*, it was the responsibility of the kinsman redeemer to carry out the punishment for the injustice done to his family member. Leviticus and Numbers are filled with the details of these laws to make sure justice was carried out swiftly and properly.

As a kinsman redeemer it was his duty as the blood avenger to bring justice when there had been bloodshed. But I believe there is more to this name than we have seen. I believe that as our avenger his purpose is to bring justice into our lives in ways that we have not seen. The first name of God given in Genesis 1 is *Elohim*, translated as Supreme God, Judge or Magistrate and Ruler of the Universe. As Magistrate He sees and weighs all sides, then brings justice into our lives. Actually, the basic intent of judgement is to make things right.

When we are wounded, hurt, confused, or afraid, our heart's cry is for someone to be there for us, to help us, to protect us, to bring justice to us. We need a righteous judge, someone to make it right. The covenant name of Jehovah found in Jeremiah is Jehovah-*Tsidkneu*, our righteousness.

> "I'll set shepherd-leaders over them who will take good care of them. They won't live in fear or panic anymore. All the lost sheep rounded up!' God's Decree. Time's coming when I'll establish a truly righteous David-Branch, A ruler who knows how to rule justly. He'll make sure of justice and keep people united. In His time Judah will be secure again and Israel will live in safety. This is the name they'll give Him: 'God-Who-Puts-Everything-Right.'" (Jeremiah 23:4-6, MSG)

What a picture of the *Go'el* as our Magistrate. Our *Go'el* will fix the injustice, repair the broken, and put everything back in right order. Sovereign authority? Yes. Righteous judge? Yes. Nurturing protector? You bet.

We seem to like that word "avenge" because most of us think we get the short end of the stick. Sometimes our loving Father allows it so that we lean on Him, run to Him, and hide under His wing. And sometimes there is a bigger picture or plan of which we are unaware. In those times we get a deeper revelation of His covenant love, His security.

When you are in a desperate place, to whom do you run? When you get angry or feel you have been wronged, where do you go? In my bitterness, I just want to get even. However, the Lord says, "Vengeance is mine," and His ways are higher than ours. He always has a plan for our redemption, good, and prosperity, but maybe it is not in our time frame nor the way we think it should look. But as your *Go'el*, He will bring justice to your situation.

Our *Go'el* does not give us only what is even; He gives us more. His name is Redeemer and He has plans to redeem the situation so you do not get what you felt you deserved—you get more. What we get is pressed down, shaken together, and running over.

Of course, at these times we too must make a choice. He has chosen to be our Kinsman Redeemer, but we must choose Him. Rather than looking to the problem or the one who caused us pain, we must choose to forgive. Not because they deserve it, but because unforgiveness in our heart is like picking up handcuffs and putting them on ourselves. By holding on to the key of bondage, we are holding on to our bitterness, resentment, and pain.

But God!

His name is "the God who sets everything right." When we choose to hide under His wing and walk in forgiveness, He gently takes the key from our hand and unlocks the chains, the handcuffs. There are no limits to His love, His power, or His might. He will move heaven and earth for you because He is in covenant with you. His promises are "Yes and amen!" His own blood, poured out in covenant, binds Him to His oath to protect and bring justice to us. He will never leave us nor forsake us. He sees us through the rainbow circle of covenant and He remembers.

"Remember" is an action word. When God remembers, movement takes place. When God remembered Hannah, she became pregnant with Samuel. When God remembered the children of Israel in Egypt, He raised up Moses as their deliverer. When God looks at you through the circle of the rainbow, He remembers covenant and great movement occurs in your life's realm. As we hide under His wings, calling on our covenant *Go'el*, He remembers and comes as a righteous judge to make it right. Looking at Psalm 18 in the Message Translation, we get an amazing picture of God's movement toward David when he cried out for help and mercy. I recommend you read this entire Psalm from the Voice or Message translation. I will share with you a few insights I received.

Early in this Psalm David was hiding behind boulders and could feel the hangman's noose around his neck. Devil waters were drowning him; death traps were everywhere; hell's ropes had him bound. But David knew and understood covenant. He understood how the shepherd would give his life for his sheep, the great lengths to which he would go to in order to protect them. He knew from where his help would come. He declared, "I love you, God; You make me strong."

Suddenly the great God, *Elohim*, the Supreme Judge of the Universe hears David as if He were the only person in the earth. Because of covenant, David got a private audience with the King Himself.

Then the Supreme Judge of the Universe arises from His throne and descends causing the earth to "wobble and lurch, and huge mountains to shake like leaves, quaking like aspen leaves because of His rage." Can you sense the earth tremble as His passion is aroused and He is consumed with jealousy for His beloved, David.

Read this physical description of Him as He comes to make everything right.

> "His nostrils flare, bellowing smoke; His mouth spits fire.
> Tongues of fire dart in and out; He lowers the sky.
> He steps down; under His feet an abyss opens up.
> He's riding a winged creature, swift on wind-wings.
> Now He's wrapped Himself in a cloak of black-cloud darkness.

> But His cloud-brightness bursts through,
> spraying hailstones and fireballs.
> Then God thundered out of heaven;
> the High God gave a great shout,
> spraying hailstones and fireballs." (Psalm 18:8-12, MSG)

What a sight to behold. Our Magistrate comes. This is what He looks like when He is on His way to take care of our enemy. Remember we do not fight against flesh and blood, but against principalities and powers. When they see the mighty Lord *Sabaoth*, the Commander of the angel armies, approaching on our behalf, our enemies flee, fall, and are defeated. He moves heaven and earth to rescue us, His beloved.

And David's response? "I stood there saved—Surprised to be loved!"

Surprised to be loved! Many times when we run to Him, hide under His covenant wing, we see ourselves as unlovable, unworthy, and unforgivable. But our *Go'el* is thrilled that we called on His name, that we remembered our covenant because He never forgets. He shows Himself strong on our behalf and surprises us with His love, His tender mercy, His grace, and His stability. That is much better than getting even. As your Kinsman Redeemer, He is your Blood Avenger, your Magistrate, who releases vengeance upon your enemy. He is the One who brings justice in the earth.

Restore from Bondage, Slavery, and Debt

> "Now if a sojourner or stranger close to you becomes rich, and *one of* your brethren who dwells by him becomes poor, and sells himself to the stranger or sojourner close to you, or to a member of the stranger's family, after he is sold he may be redeemed again. One of his brothers may redeem him; or his uncle or his uncle's son may redeem him; or anyone who is near of kin to him in his family may redeem him; or if he is able he may redeem himself." (Lev. 25:47-49)

The Law of the Kinsman Redeemer, the Go'el

We have all sold ourselves to the slavery of sin, but Jesus, the Kinsman Redeemer said,

"Most assuredly, I say to you, whoever commits sin is a slave of sin. And a slave does not abide in the house forever, but a son abides forever. Therefore if the Son makes you free, you shall be free indeed" (John 8: 34-36)

At the time of the giving of Torah, when the Law of Redemption was clearly defined to Israel, slavery was a part of the culture. In the wilderness after receiving Torah, they stood between the two mountains as Moses read the blessings and curses of Torah aloud. The Israelites had the freedom once again to choose life or the curses of disobedience and death. They cried out, "All you have said we will do." They had been held in slavery for four hundred years and were ready to be free. One of the freedoms they could now enjoy was celebrating Sabbath. As my friend Norma says, slaves work every day with no day of rest. It is a good thing to remember on Sabbath, the Jews are no longer slaves!

A slave is a person who is owned and controlled by another. They are considered property, have no rights, and are strictly at the mercy of their owner. They cannot choose where they live, what they do for work or how they are used or abused. They receive no remuneration for their labor. Ownership and control are the key issues in slavery. Slavery comes in many forms but all go back to the root issue of sin and death. Jesus said He came to give us life abundantly, yet He never takes away our freedom to choose.

Most of us feel far removed from this type of physical slavery. Yet our wrong choices bring us back into bondage of another sort. Our Creator longs for us to love Him freely because He first loved us. He designed us for a destiny of freedom, a destiny of hope, and a good future. His Father heart grieves for us when we yield to the father of lies who has come to enslave us, to control us, and take away our freedom. He does this through fear, addiction to drugs, alcohol or pornography, rejection, woundedness, and the list could go on. We are enslaved any time we are controlled by another, be it a human or a demonic spirit. The bottom line here is that we, like Adam and Eve, make wrong choices and become enslaved by our own sin. And just like Adam and Eve and the nation of Israel, we have to be bought back and delivered from the slavery of our choices. The cost is high. The cost is the sacrifice of covenant.

Jesus stated His purpose for coming to the earth in His first public appearance in a small synagogue in Nazareth. He took the scroll and read from Isaiah. "The Spirit of the Lord is upon me." In my own words: "The creative *ruach* breath, the breath that breathed life into Adam, the breath of *El Elyon* the Supreme Creator, has commissioned Me, *Yeshua*, to come down from My glorious throne as your Brother, your near Kinsman to heal your broken hearts, bring you out of all slavery, to buy you back, and set you free. I came to restore your sight, your physical and spiritual sight, so that you can see your Father's goodness and feel His love once again."

Are you a slave to habitual sin? Jesus sets you free. Are you a slave to fear and insecurity? Jesus sets you free. Are you a slave to doubt and unbelief? Jesus sets you free. 1 Corinthians 5:17 reminds us:

> "Therefore, if anyone is in Christ, he is a new creation; old things have passed away; behold, all things have become new."

We are slaves no longer because the blood of the Lamb, our Kinsman Redeemer has come to buy us back and set us free.

Restore the Property and Inheritance

> "If one of your brethren becomes poor, and has sold some of his possession, and if his redeeming relative [*go'el*] comes to redeem it, then he may redeem what his brother sold" (Lev. 25:25).

The Law of the Kinsman Redeemer, the Go'el

In Israel property and inheritance were restored every fifty years in the Year of Jubilee. Each family was to go back to their original family land and reclaim what had been stolen or lost during the past fifty years. Since land sales were only valid until the next Jubilee, the price was set accordingly.

However, it could also be bought back before the fifty-year Jubilee by the kinsman redeemer. We see this clearly in the story of Ruth and Boaz. As the *go'el*, Boaz purchased back the property that had belonged to Naomi's dead husband Elimelech, which was her inheritance.

When Adam sinned in the garden he became an orphan with no inheritance, no portion, and no hope of a righteous destiny. Jesus, the hope of glory, paid the full price to bring Adam's race, us, back into our full inheritance regaining what was lost. We became fully adopted sons and His future bride with the grace to receive the inheritance God has deposited in us and in our bloodlines. No longer widows with no inheritance, we became fully adopted sons and daughters and His future bride with a full inheritance restored.

At the Fall in the Garden we were not the only losers. Our Father lost His inheritance of sons and daughters, He lost the inheritance of the nations, and He lost the beauty of all creation. The only one qualified to redeem it all back was our brother Jesus, as a near kinsman who came as flesh and blood. He was the only one with the authority and anointing to restore and buy back the inheritance of both the Father and the widow. He willingly gave up His riches in glory not only to buy back our inheritance, but also to regain and buy back all of creation for His Father. Covenant works for the benefit of both the covenanter and the one with whom he is making covenant.

My friends, Charlotte and Roger Merschbrock of Jubilee Destiny Ministries, have written an incredible little book called *Our Jubilee, Your Destiny* that is chock full of the blessings of your inheritance. I'd like to share a portion of those with you,

> According to Psalm 16:5 and 6, the land is your portion and your cup. He maintains your portion and the lines have fallen

to you in pleasant places. Do not be like Esau who despised his inheritance, but through obedience and worship you will own and steward it according to His call on your life.

One of the roots of lost inheritance is unbelief from your carnal father Adam. "Has God really said?" When we look to see who we are, what we have or do not have, we begin to doubt that God really said He would release our inheritance to us. Our enemy has come to steal, kill, and destroy our identity, our portion, and our destiny. One way he does this is to cause us to doubt the goodness of God and to doubt God really desires to pour out His blessings on us.

One-third of the priests' work was to bless. Think about it. This means twenty minutes out of every hour should be spent in blessing. One-third of our day should be spent releasing His blessings to our home, our family, our friends and even blessing ourselves. But we look around us and, if we do not see the blessing materialize, we doubt His goodness and move into doubt and unbelief. This was what the children of Israel did in the wilderness when they complained to Moses.

"We have no water. We have no food. It's too hot. It's too cold. Did He bring us here to die?"

But God!

He gave them fresh water from the rock. He gave them quail in the desert. He shaded them with the cloud by day and kept them warm with the fire by night. Not just because of His love for them. He was bound by His word, His covenant, signed by His blood. In His covenant He vowed to provide for them, protect them, and love them. He would be their husband and all that it entailed, because His promises are eternal and forever. He fulfilled every last word. In the same way He is committed to us. Jesus cut a covenant with us and He will fulfill every last word.

Acts 17:26-27 explains He has set our boundaries so we and our children will seek Him and find Him. He has promised to enlarge our borders and release inheritance to our children, spiritual and natural. They will come back into their borders that were established for them according to our covenant with Him. I call on my *Go'el* for this portion of my inheritance daily. It is my deepest desire for my children and grandchildren to follow the Lord with all of their hearts and to fulfill their destiny that was set for them. My children will inherit nations because He has plans for their good and not evil. He will give them a hope and a future, a very good future. These are conditions and provisions of my covenant according to Isaiah 54 and Jeremiah 29:11. This is my inheritance because I am grafted into the covenant of Abraham. You too may claim this inheritance for yourself and your children. This is a generational covenant, secured by the blood sacrifice of your Kinsman Redeemer.

Recently I have become interested in my ancestry and it has been amazing to see pictures of my sixth great-grandfather, Daniel Carroll, who came from Ireland. In both my mother and father's bloodlines I have been astounded at the number of teachers, preachers, and government officials who loved the Lord. I hear many Christians talk about the blessings and curses of bloodlines. I believe I am walking in the blessings of my bloodlines that were released to me as my ancestors worshiped and obeyed God. I can be assured that as I walk in obedience I will increase these blessings for my children and grandchildren. That is inheritance restored and released. This is part of our covenant with our *Go'el*.

There is a marvelous picture of inheritance released through worship and obedience in Numbers 25. Take a look at Phinehas, one of my heroes in the wilderness. God's promise to Phinehas was dramatic, mind-boggling, and generational.

Remember the story when the Israelites sinned with the neighboring Moabites? They were told not to fraternize with the locals or else they would suffer the consequences. The Message Bible says it like this:

> "It started when the Moabite women invited the Israeli men to their sex-and-religion worship. They ate together and then

worshiped their gods. Israel ended up joining in the worship of the Baal of Peor" (Numbers 25:1-8 MSG).

God saw their disobedience and sent a plague that was moving rapidly throughout the camp. Folks were dying by the thousands, twenty-four thousand to be exact. As the people were weeping and crying to the Lord, out of the shadows steps Phinehas, the hero of the day. This quiet priest came tearing out of the tabernacle with javelin in hand. Running swiftly though the camp he came to the tent of Zimri and drove a spear through the heart of both Zimri and Cozbi, the daughter a Midianite tribal chief. Suddenly the plague stopped.

The King of Creation took notice and spoke.

"Because Phinehas was zealous (*a burning passionate jealousy on behalf of someone deeply loved*) for my honor, tell him that I am making a Covenant-of-Peace with him. He and his descendants are joined in a covenant of eternal priesthood" (Numbers 25:11-13, MSG).

This one act of passion, zeal, and honor shifted Phinehas from behind the scenes and unknown to a greatly honored man in the nation of Israel. God had increased his boundaries, shifted his borders, expanded his sphere of influence. He became known for his exceptional wisdom in understanding the ways of the Lord.

When Moses sent the army to war, Phinehas was honored to carry the holy articles of the Tabernacle and the signal trumpets in his hand.

When the leaders of Israel had to figure out what was going on across the river with the Tribes of Reuben, Gad, and the half Tribe of Manasseh, they trusted Phinehas as mediator to decide whether to embrace or kill them.

When Israel had major issues with the Tribe of Benjamin, the leaders called on Phinehas to make the decision to go to war.

Phinehas was the one trusted to be over all of the gatekeepers, because the Lord was with him. This meant he was the ultimate authority over who came and went within the gates of the Tabernacle and nation. The passion, character, and wisdom of Phinehas were astounding.

The Law of the Kinsman Redeemer, the Go'el

It was this passion that also released immense inheritance to his children and grandchildren. In looking down his family line we find these noteworthy priests: Zadok, the who helped King David inaugurate worship twenty-four hours a day in the Tabernacle in Jerusalem; Azariah who was Solomon's priest in the first Temple; Ezra, the exiled priest who was assigned to rebuild Jerusalem after the Babylonian captivity; and Eleazar, who was trusted to weigh the silver and gold in the temple.

All of these men had one common ancestor: Phinehas.

What an amazing picture of inheritance received and inheritance released in a remarkable and phenomenal way.

Isn't this what we want? To receive the fullness of our inheritance and to release more of His passion, honor, and love to our children and their children? God is a generational, covenant-keeping God who remembers the covenant in your bloodline and releases your inheritance with great mercy and grace generationally.

Go back and study what inheritance has been lost in your bloodline. Then approach the Lord in worship and remind Him of your covenant. Ask for restoration of all that was stolen from your bloodline through sin and disobedience. Confess the iniquity which has caused the blessings intended for you and your generations to be thwarted and held back. Above all, make sure you are not continuing to walk in that same iniquity. Then choose to walk in obedience, integrity, and honor, allowing Him to begin to release the treasure chest of blessings meant for your family line. He came to restore your inheritance. He is your *Go'el*.

Jesus, the great *Go'el*, fulfilled every portion of His duties with zeal, love, and power. He came to marry us, to set us free and deliver us, to bring justice to our lives. We are His bride and He is cleansing us, bringing purity to our lives so that we will be without spot or blemish, prepared for our wedding feast when He comes to claim us as His own. He is the *Go'el*. He is the Covenant Keeper.

Chapter Five
The Five Women in Matthew

When God wanted to change the world, He sent a baby. In the book of Matthew there are forty-two generations carefully listed, from Abraham to the birth of Jesus, each naming the father of the next generation. But there are five women's names inserted here and there. Why these particular women and not Sarah or Leah or Rachel? At first, the women mentioned seemed rather random to me: Tamar, widowed twice and thought to be the cause of her husbands' deaths; Rahab, a Canaanite prostitute; Ruth, a detestable Moabite; Bathsheba, the questionable wife of King David; Mary, a sweet, gentle young virgin, really the only one who seemed to be worthy of the honor of mention in the bloodline of the Messiah. Yet some of the most wondrous and poignant pictures of the Kinsman Redeemer, the *Go'el*, are found in the stories of these five remarkable women.

We know Jehovah is very intentional, never random in His actions. Clearly He is meticulous in recording the generations and bloodlines of His people because bloodlines carry destiny. From Adam to Abraham, David to Jesus, this bloodline carried the destiny to release kings and ultimately the King of all kings.

Why these particular women? My friend, Norma Sarvis, made a statement to me I will never forget: "God was looking for a womb." I would add "and a hungry heart."

In the beginning, God set in motion a natural order in the earth of male and female. As He designed His plan for redemption, He introduced and incorporated the Law of the *Go'el* as a way to redeem the house of Adam, the house of death. Another portion of that plan was to use the natural law of conception and birth to bring about this redemption. Women were designed to partner in a way with the Creator of life to create, nurture, protect, and then bring forth birth. In His plan for the nation of Israel, He used these five women to birth His redemptive plan for Adam's race. Tamar conceived and birthed the Tribe of Judah, known as the *Go'el* Tribe. Rahab protected this growing seed while Ruth's marriage to Boaz brought a clear and stunning picture of the *Go'el* Marriage. Bathsheba birthed the bloodline of the kings of Judah and Mary, partnering in the most unique way, actually birthed the *Go'el* in the flesh.

As we look more closely at each one of their stories and the circumstances surrounding the birth of their sons, we get a deeper understanding of His covenant plan to send a *go'el* to bring about His plan of redemption.

In order to protect them from the law and culture in which they lived, Tamar, Rahab, Ruth, Bathsheba, and Mary all needed a man to step up and marry them, protecting their lives and His inheritance. Each needed to come under his *tallit* of covenant to protect them from dishonor or even death. Tamar, Bathsheba, and Mary were pregnant without husbands and according to the law of the day should have been stoned. Rahab was a Canaanite prostitute and Ruth a widowed Moabite with no means of support. Neither of these Gentile women could obtain an inheritance according to the Law of Israel. Each woman was uncovered in some fashion. In each instance, God provided a man, a type of kinsman redeemer, who would provide a covering for these women.

Yet none of them walked in a victim spirit nor were they passive in their situations. As stated above, God was looking for a womb, a woman with a willing heart into which He could pour His passion, His purpose, and His power. He found these five women. The Lord allowed events to transpire so He could show Himself strong on their behalf, each event revealing more of His nature as a Redeemer. He provided a way of inheritance for them as His daughters. Let's take a look at their stories for a deeper appreciation of our phenomenal God and the honor He bestows on women who look to Him for redemption.

Tamar

Tamar was chosen by God to bring forth the Tribe of Judah from whom the Messiah would come. Her name means to be erect, a palm tree. Palm trees are quite different than any other tree on the earth. These trees bend and sway with the winds so they are not uprooted, broken, or blown over. Although their roots don't stretch out very far or deep, there are a lot of them and they have the same flexibility as the trunks with a whole lot of gripping power. This describes Tamar. She was married to two wretched, evil men, widowed twice, abandoned, deserted, and deceived by her father-in-law in order to keep her from receiving her rightful inheritance. She then prostituted herself, became pregnant, and was threatened with being burned alive because of her pregnancy. In spite of these strong winds of adversity this palm tree of a woman gripped tighter, bent deeper, and triumphed over it all.

Of course, there was no nation of Israel during this time in history. Tamar was a Canaanite and Scripture never says if she was a believer in Jehovah *Elohim*. However, I believe if she was not in the beginning, as she saw Him work on her behalf, she became one. We do know she was smart, wise, and kept her head in a crisis. Actually, Tamar was an amazing woman of character. I know women like that today. Sometimes they appear pushy and strong, but they have a focus toward God that will not be denied. Tamar was willing to push through to grasp her inheritance. She knew her destiny was more than to die as a widow in her father's house. From this strong-willed, courageous woman came a line of kings including King David and the Lion of the Tribe of Judah, the King of Kings Himself.

Most of the time we prefer the story of Ruth because of the love and beauty portrayed there. We see Tamar as a victim of circumstances, caught in the middle of deception, lust, and sex. Yet in spite of this scandalous state of affairs, the story of Tamar is actually one of hope, courage, and bravery.

Tamar needed a kinsman redeemer. She needed a husband to buy her back, redeem her, and release her inheritance. She needed justice. Although this story occurred long before the law was given in Exodus, the kinsman redeemer edict was clearly in place. It was common law during this time for the brother to marry the widow so that the dead brother's inheritance could be carried on. Judah reluctantly became her *go'el* and married her becoming her kinsman redeemer. But it was God who redeemed the situation and brought the justice necessary for her to come into the fullness of her destiny.

We know the story of Tamar's marriages to Er and then to Onan, his brother, who was to be her first *go'el*. God makes it very clear both of these men were so evil that He killed them because of their wickedness. Judah did not give Tamar to his son, Shelah, for fear that he would die too. There is historical thought that because of the level of iniquity of these men, God could not allow them to be in the bloodline of Messiah. Scripture does not say that the third son, Shelah, was just as detestable, but it does indicate God's hand was strong in preserving His own bloodline, the bloodline of the Messiah.

Realizing Judah's deception toward her, Tamar shrewdly came up with a plan. She posed as a prostitute, tricked Judah, and became pregnant with his sons. As Judah was about to have her judged, she proved to Him that she was carrying his children. Judah was humbled, realizing this was the hand of the Lord against him because of his deception and injustice toward Tamar. Tamar was vindicated.

Judah had reluctantly fulfilled the role of the *go'el*, the kinsman redeemer for Tamar. Perez, whose name means the one who breaks open the way, was born as a child of this redemption causing the Tribe of Judah to be forever linked with a *go'el*, becoming known as the *Go'el* Tribe. From there we see four more instances of a *go'el* stepping into the bloodline of Jesus, assuring that the destiny of Abraham's bloodline was never lost. Finally the great *Go'el*, Jesus, the Messiah Himself, would step into history, not only to redeem the Tribe of Judah, but also to redeem the nation of Israel, the nations of the world, and, in fact, all of creation. What a picture of redemption Jehovah had begun to paint.

When we hear the name Tamar, we remember God's intent and purpose cannot be frustrated, regardless of lust, wickedness, evil, deception or iniquity. More than that, we appreciate and embrace the truth that He can redeem willing hearts from those circumstances and even use them for good in our lives according to Romans 8:28. The Lord chose this bent down palm tree of a woman and raised her up to stand tall among champions to accomplish His destiny for her life and protect His bloodline. Tamar helped birth a nation.

Why is Tamar in Matthew? She was the first recorded widow redeemed by a go'el in the bloodline of our Great *Go'el*. God moved on Tamar's behalf and she became the mother of twins. The first was Perez whose name means "The one who breaks open the way." Her second son was Zerah whose name means "The rising light." She raised them as sons of the covenant, building the *Go'el* Tribe, the Tribe of Judah. Even in these earliest generations of Abraham their names point to the Lion of the Tribe of Judah, who is the risen light and who breaks open the way for us to step into covenant.

Rahab

Whereas Tamar helped to conceive and birth the *Go'el* Tribe, Rahab partnered with God to protect it.

> "By an act of faith, Rahab, the Jericho harlot, welcomed the spies and escaped the destruction that came on those who refused to trust God." (Hebrews 11:31, MSG).

"The same with Rahab, the Jericho harlot. Wasn't her action in hiding God's spies and helping them escape—that seamless unity of believing and doing—what counted with God?" (James 2:25, MSG).

Rahab was caught in a shift of power. The great God of the Hebrews was moving in miraculous ways in the earth and her city, Jericho, was soon to be overthrown by this advancing Hebrew nation. Transition was on the horizon. She had heard about the God of Israel, how He parted the Red Sea and defeated armies who dared to fight against them. Possibly there was a longing in her heart for more, but how would this Canaanite prostitute shift out of what was known and comfortable into the unknown. God saw her heart. He moves to and fro in the earth looking for hungry hearts and He found one in Rahab.

As mentioned before, God is very intentional and meticulous about His bloodline. Jehovah had plans for Rahab long before she knew Him. She was destined to be a mother of Zion, to be in the very lineage of His Son, the Messiah.

Her everyday life in Jericho does not necessarily reflect such a profound destiny. She was born into the male-dominated society of Canaan, a wicked nation of idolaters where she survived as a harlot or prostitute. Her name means "to make room, to open" (*Strong's Exhaustive Concordance* #H7337). As a young girl did she have dreams of a happy home with lots of children running around? Or did she always have to push, trying to make a place for herself because there was no one to champion her? Our God is *El Roi*, the God who sees. He saw Rahab, heard her hungry heart's cry, and answered it triumphantly. He gave her an opportunity to step out in faith on what she had heard. However, in doing so she put her very life in danger.

How did the Hebrew spies find the one woman in the city of Jericho with a hungry heart who would hide them and even lie to the king to protect them? Simple for God. Her house just happened to be on the wall of this mighty, fortified city, an easy exit for the spies. Coincidence? Acts 17:26 tells us He sets our times and seasons and designates the exact places we should live. Therefore, we can rest assured this "great God of the Hebrews," as Rahab called Him, put her in the right place at the right time at the right season of change in the earth. Remember, He does that for us too.

We are told in the books of Hebrews and James that Rahab was saved because of her faith. She believed and took the leap. In that moment of decision, she trusted in this unknown God and everything shifted. This harlot was embraced by the Hebrew nation, became a national hero, and is mentioned by name three times in the New Testament.

But why is she in the bloodline of Messiah? Could it be that God saw in Rahab the tenacity to face death and trust in Him? Did her courageous faith amaze Him and touch something deep in His heart, just as the faith of a Gentile centurion would amaze Jesus when He was on earth? Did God need for this generational blessing to be released into its fullness in His own son? I would answer with a resounding "Yes!"

After the fall of Jericho, Rahab remained in the camp of Israel and was honored as a hero because she had protected the spies. But God saw there was more for her. There is always more with God. Her indomitable spirit and faith would be important to those coming after her, so God brought a mighty warrior named Salmon to marry her. Although he was not a kinsman, Salmon's name means "a cover, or a mantle," (*Strong's Exhaustive Concordance* #H8008, H8071). He is known as the "Father of Bethlehem," which would become known as the *Go'el* City. By spreading his mantle or *tallit* to cover her, He stood in the stead of a redeemer, bringing her into the *Go'el* Tribe of Judah. Rahab, this Gentile woman with no inheritance in the land, received her rich inheritance as a daughter of Zion in the bloodline of the Messiah because of Salmon.

Again there is more. As we note the kindness of Boaz to Ruth, his faithfulness to God, and his extraordinary grace to embrace a Moabite woman bringing her into covenant, we know Rahab taught her son well. Her story prepared him to be the kinsman redeemer for Ruth. Yes, this great God of the Hebrews made room for Rahab.

Ruth

This amazing woman is listed right in the middle of the five women in Matthew 1. Every element of the *Go'el* Law of Redemption was portrayed as Boaz, the son of Rahab, born in Bethlehem, stepped onto the stage of history for us to see a magnificent image of Jesus, our great *Go'el*.

The Book of Ruth embodies the compassionate heart of Jehovah. In this narrative we see the Torah in action as it protected the most vulnerable in Israel: the poor through the Law of Gleaning; the widow and orphan through the Law of Inheritance and the Law of the *Go'el*.

Because bloodlines are so important to God, we must note the lineage of Naomi. Elimelech, husband of Naomi and a member of the *Go'el* Tribe of Judah, left Bethlehem to immigrate to Moab because of famine. His two sons marry Moabite women, Ruth and Orpah. All three men die, so the three women become widows. Unlike Israel, it appears there were no laws in the land of Moab to take care of widows, but Naomi knew that she would be cared for in in Israel. She may have had a concern about the two Moabite girls, so she encouraged them both to go back to their fathers' homes. Orpah chose to go back but Ruth embraced the God of Israel and returned with Naomi to Bethlehem, the "house of bread."

There is an interesting side note here about the choices made by Ruth and Orpah. Our choices affect our destinies. Both of these women were carrying the seed of champions. We know that Ruth was the great, grandmother of David, but according to tradition, Orpah was the great, grandmother of Goliath, the enemy of David. Here we see yet again how our choices affect not only us, but also our children and our children's children. Bloodline curses or blessings: our choice.

Another often overlooked note is there was a curse at play between the Moabites and the Israelites.

> "An Ammonite or Moabite shall not enter the assembly of the Lord; even to the tenth generation none of his descendants shall enter the assembly of the Lord forever, because they did not meet you with bread and water on the road when you came out of Egypt" (Deut. 5:3-4).

This could have posed a problem for future generations, including King David. However, Ruth, as a Moabite, actually provided bread for Naomi, an Israelite, in the City of Bread. By coming in the opposite spirit of this curse, Ruth released a blessing instead. Another right choice that affected future generations.

Boaz was a wealthy landowner from the *Go'el* Tribe of Judah, a kinsman of Elimelech. Naomi understood the Law of Gleaning which stated that the landowner was to reap the field with only one pass in order to leave grain for the widows and the poor. Just my speculation here, but perhaps she had heard of Boaz's reputation as a kind man and knew his mother was Rahab, the Jericho harlot. Hoping this would give Ruth more favor in his field, she told Ruth to glean there. We do know that when Boaz came to check on his field, he was drawn to Ruth when he was told of her kindness toward her mother-in-law Naomi.

When she heard how kind Boaz had been to Ruth, Naomi, knowing the laws of the *go'el* and inheritance, explained to Ruth their next course of action. Ruth was to approach Boaz while he was sleeping on the threshing floor and because he was a near kinsman, ask him to cover her with his skirt. She was invoking her right under the laws of Israel, asking for the covenant covering of his *tallit*, in essence asking him to redeem her as her *go'el*.

Boaz, a man of integrity who knew the law, realized there was a closer kinsman than he. Inheritance and redemption were of the utmost importance, so it had to be carried out to the letter of the law.

Remember, when a widow requested to invoke the Law of the *Go'el*, the kinsman redeemer was never under obligation to do so. It had to be his choice. The three qualifications were

- He had to be qualified as a kinsman
- He had to have the resources to do it
- He had to be willing to do it

Boaz met the second and third of these requirements and quickly took measures to remedy the situation to meet the first requirement. He found the nearer kinsman, met with him at the gates of the city, the place of government, and addressed the issue of redemption. Actually it was Naomi and Ruth's portion to do this, but Boaz assumed the full responsibility and with great wisdom and finesse took care of the matter.

Ruth and Naomi are a wonderful picture of Jew and Gentile walking together to accomplish the fullness of Jehovah's plan in the earth. Both women needed Boaz, their kinsman redeemer, just as both Jew and Gentile need Jesus as our Kinsman Redeemer.

Their offspring, Obed, was both Jew and Gentile, an awesome picture of the One New Man spoken of in the book of Ephesians.

All of this took place in Bethlehem, the House of Bread where the Bread of Life would be born. Bethlehem, known as the city of the *Go'el*.

"But you, Bethlehem, David's country, the runt of the litter. From you will come the leader who will shepherd-rule Israel. He will be no upstart, no pretender. His family tree is ancient and distinguished" (Micah 5:2, MSG).

Bathsheba

It was easy to see the *go'el* in each of the lives of the other four women in Matthew chapter one, but Bathsheba caused me to stop and re-examine my premise that these women all had a type of kinsman redeemer. I had seen the movies and heard the stories of Bathsheba as an adulteress or a manipulative seductress. Many commentaries of the Old Testament blamed both David and Bathsheba for the events found in II Samuel. Some even put most of the blame on her.

Early one morning after several days of research I simply asked the Lord, "How did you see Bathsheba?" He quickly responded, "As a gentle lamb." This did not fit my paradigm nor did it fit the papers and commentaries I had been reading. I re-read the story of David and Bathsheba. How could I have missed it all of these years? God's heart for this often-misunderstood and maligned woman was straightforward and crystal clear. He saw her as a gentle lamb. He made sure that it was recorded through the words of Nathan the prophet:

> "The poor man had only one little female lamb that he had bought. He raised her, and she grew up in his home with his children. She would eat his food and drink from his cup. She rested in his arms and was like a daughter" (II Samuel 12:3, GW).

Remember, God is intentional in recording the lives of the people in the Bible. If there was sin in their lives, He made sure it was recorded. As I read the account in II Samuel, I was broken hearted for this one who has been blamed for centuries for sins that were not her doing. If anyone needed redemption, justice, and retribution it was Bathsheba.

God stepped in, sending Nathan the prophet and Ahithophel, Bathsheba's grandfather, as her protectors and avengers. Nathan not only carried God's word as an advisor to the king, but also carried God's heart for Bathsheba over the remaining lifetime of King David.

The story begins, "In the spring, the time when kings go out to battle, David sent Joab ..."

Where was David when he should have been in the field with his men? He was on his rooftop, restless, unable to sleep. He was missing the camaraderie of his mighty men. David had the heart of a warrior.

While the men with whom he had fought and won many battles were sleeping on a hard ground, he lay in his clean bed and could have the company of any of his several wives or a concubine of his choice. Unlike Rahab who had been in the right place at the right time, King David was in the wrong place at the wrong time, which led to fitful, disturbed, sleepless nights.

David knew Bathsheba well. She was younger than the king and possibly grew up right before his eyes. Her grandfather, Ahithophel, was an advisor to King David. Her father, Eliam and her husband, Uriah, were counted among his mighty men. Perhaps King David had danced at his friend Uriah's wedding.

David had so many choices, yet he was drawn to Bathsheba. Was it her purity that caught his eye and his heart? Her name means daughter of the oath and she was loved deeply by her grandfather and Nathan the prophet. What we do know is that when a king, with the power of life and death at his command, summoned one to his palace, there was little choice but to go.

As Bathsheba was escorted to the palace that evening, she was possibly a little confused. David was a friend of her husband and her father who were out on the battlefield. Had something happened to one of them? Why else would the king, her family friend, come to get her in the night?

Surprised? Maybe. Willing? I doubt it. Shamed? Most likely. Raped? Don't know.

What we do know is that God was displeased with David, not Bathsheba. And so were Ahithophel and Nathan, which we will see later as the consequences played out over the following months and years.

Because of David's lust and disobedience to the law, upon learning that Bathsheba was pregnant, he tried to cover up his sin with yet a more heinous one: murder. In most kingdoms of the day, the king made laws as he saw fit, many times exempting himself. But this was not just any kingdom. This was the kingdom of Israel where Jehovah

El Roi, who sees and knows the heart, actually ruled and reigned. His Law, the Torah, was the law of the land. David knew this law, but in his blindness he forgot that even as king, he must answer to God.

When confronted by Nathan the prophet he was shocked and grieved at how he had walked in unrighteousness. Quick repentance brought forgiveness and restoration of his tender heart, but it did not stop the consequences.

Bathsheba, the innocent one, required justice because of this wrong done to her. Of all these five women, she needed the avenger to come and bring public justice to vindicate her before the nation. Following the loss of her baby, she went into mourning and possibly walked in shame. Our enemy uses shame as a weapon against us, especially when we have been violated in this way.

I would like to say here, if you have been victimized through sexual abuse, you can identify with Bathsheba. If so, cry out to your *Go'el*, your Kinsman Redeemer for His justice and healing. He will make a way for you.

But God saw Bathsheba's broken and shamed heart as did her grandfather Ahithophel and Nathan the prophet. As to public vindication, Nathan publicly proclaimed the Word of the Lord to King David:

> "You are the man! Now therefore, the sword shall never depart from your house, because you have despised Me, and have taken the wife of Uriah the Hittite to be your wife." Thus says the Lord: "Behold, I will raise up adversity against you from your own house; and I will take your wives before your eyes and give them to your neighbor, and he shall lie with your wives in the sight of this sun. For you did it secretly, but I will do this thing before all Israel, before the sun." (II Samuel 12:7,10-12)

Shortly following Nathan's confrontation the consequences prophesied began to happen. Tamar, David's daughter, was raped by her half-brother, Ammon. When David refused to hold Ammon accountable for this dishonorable act, Tamar's brother Absalom became enraged and bitter toward his father. After he had killed Ammon, Absalom escaped the city and began to plot a civil war against David.

Bathsheba's grandfather, Ahithophel, stepped into the role of avenger to publicly hold David accountable for what he had done to Bathsheba. Although He could not openly accuse the King of the violation of His granddaughter, he found a way. He became an advisor to Absalom and encouraged him to bring out David's concubines to the rooftop and publically raped them when Absalom seized David's throne in Jerusalem, fulfilling the prophetic word from Nathan to David thirteen years earlier. The sword of the Lord never departed from David's house because of his wicked sin against God and against Bathsheba.

However, David's heart was also broken over what he had done as we can discern in Psalm 51. From this point in his life, David shifted his focus toward receiving forgiveness from the Lord. Remembering the days of his youth as a shepherd, he rose to become known as the shepherd king. Overwhelmed by such grace and mercy, he pursued the Lord with all of his heart, worshiping Him with abandonment. David instituted glorious worship with trained musicians and singers and the splendor and glory of the Lord could be heard throughout the city of Jerusalem during David's reign.

David, like all of us, was a sinner. But he served a wondrous, awesome God, full of mercy and compassion who forgives, restores, and redeems us. David, too, needed a redeemer and he found Him in Jehovah.

And Bathsheba? Nathan championed Bathsheba the rest of his life. Seeing her through the eyes of the Lord as a gentle lamb he protected her. As a wise prophet and counselor, Nathan saw to it that at the end of David's life it was her son, Solomon, who sat on the throne and that Bathsheba became the most important woman in the kingdom, the Queen Mother.

Yes, I believe Bathsheba had a type of kinsman redeemer. Although David married her, redeeming her inheritance as a widow, God raised up two men who took the responsibility of avenger. One was her grandfather who publicly avenged the wrong done to her; the other was a mighty prophet who was unafraid to confront a king in defense of an innocent lamb.

Through all of her trials in early years, Bathsheba learned to trust in the Lord, listen to Nathan, and walk in great wisdom. When her son, Solomon ascended the throne, he honored her as his closest advisor. King Solomon sought the Lord, asked for wisdom and became known as the wisest man in the earth. Could his request have been influenced by Nathan and Bathsheba? I don't know, but it is a possibility.

Some believe one of the Solomon's names was Lemuel (*Strongs*, #H3927). The first verses of Proverbs 31 begins, "The words of King Lemuel, the strong advice his mother gave Him." Were these Bathsheba's own standards as she supported and remained loyal to King David the remainder of his life? Of all of David's wives, he chose Bathsheba's son to be the heir to his throne. Obviously David's heart trusted in her as detailed in Proverbs 31.

As mentioned earlier, lust, sin, and wickedness cannot thwart the plans of the Lord and certainly Bathsheba's life is yet another picture of His faithfulness to bring justice and inheritance to His bride.

Mary, the Woman Jehovah Trusted

All of the women we have discussed were widowed except Rahab, who although not widowed, still needed a Jewish husband to bring her into her inheritance in Israel. In every occasion, God brought a male redeemer to avenge and cover them, bringing them into the covenant of Abraham.

Mary's story is totally different, yet vital in bringing forth the *Go'el*, the Kinsman Redeemer of Israel. She was the virgin spoken of in Isaiah.

"So the Lord Himself will give you this sign: a virgin will become pregnant and give birth to a son, and she will name Him Immanuel, meaning God is with us." (Isaiah 7:14)

"But when the fullness of time had come, God sent forth His Son, born of a woman, born under the law, to redeem those who were under the law." (Gal. 4:4)

"In the fullness of time ..." Mary was born in the right place at the right time with the right lineage and the right heart. Jehovah had spent over four thousand years planning for this single moment in time. He had created the earth on the third day and designated the place for His Son to be born. He, likewise, created the very hill, called The Skull, where this same Son would die. Nothing random here. On the fourth day, He set the heavens in motion and designated the time set for the Star of Bethlehem to appear in the heavens. On the sixth day He created lambs. And He created the lions, both symbolic of His Son. All designed for this single moment: The fullness of time.

There have been libraries dedicated to Mary and so much is known about her. I want to look at the circumstance surrounding her conception of the Messiah. I want to see how Joseph stepped in as her earthly redeemer, yet another picture of God's kindness and honor for this woman. God was watching Mary from the time He created her in her mother's womb, waiting for the fullness of time.

Jehovah saw in her a heart He could trust. Mary's name, Miriam in Hebrew, comes from myrrh, a bitter herb that when crushed releases a sweet fragrance. This herb is the basis of the most expensive perfumes and was also used as a burial herb to anoint the dead.

Think about it. Mary, a lovely young Hebrew girl from a good family with lots of promise becomes pregnant and she is not married. Grounds for stoning. How difficult it must have been for her, knowing the law of the land. But by God's grace and mercy she was able to walk with her head held high, because she knew the truth of this matter. She knew she was chosen. Mary, the woman God trusted.

Her name suggests that to walk in this much grace was costly, just like the perfumes made from myrrh. But in the crushing, a sweet fragrance was released to the world: Jesus, the Messiah. His grace was sufficient for her throughout her life as His mother. Truly a sword pierced her heart as she walked through the heartache of watching her son die on that brutal cross. Yes, she endured much crushing, but the heartache turned to joy at His resurrection when the fragrance of new life was released.

There were two hearts Jehovah trusted to usher in His son. Following an angelic encounter, Joseph would also share the secret that would change all of creation. Joseph, an honorable man, full of integrity, stepped into the gap of the culture to marry Mary, who was pregnant with another's child. They were already betrothed, legally committed to each other for marriage, but their wedding day had not arrived. At that time in their society she could have been stoned or, at the very least, disgraced before the community. She would have become an outcast, as would her child. Even after they married they had to face their friends and neighbors from the small town of Nazareth -- people who believed they hadn't waited for their wedding. This in itself was a difficult thing for a righteous man like Joseph to bear; yet he did so without a word of explanation to anyone. He was willing to be Mary's earthly partner, save her reputation, and possibly her life.

As we look a little closer at these two, we find they took their responsibilities very seriously. Honoring Jehovah by keeping the laws of Judaism passed down from generation to generation through the Torah, they were faithful and obedient to do all that was required of Jewish parents. They dedicated the baby at the temple and went through the purification rites for Mary. When He was twelve years old, they brought Him again to the Temple for His Bar Mitzvah. No, Mary was not a widow, nor was Joseph a kinsman, yet he was willing to cover her with his *tallit,* the covering of covenant, safeguarding their secret that Jesus truly was the Son of God.

It has been said, "We are defined, not by the words we say, but by the choices we make." This young Hebrew couple made the choice to trust Jehovah. Once the choice was made Mary and Joseph were caught up in a drama which would unfold in surprising ways: a trip to Bethlehem near the end of the pregnancy; trouble finding a place for the baby to be born; the visit of the shepherds and their tales of the angels; the wealthy magi who financed their hurried escape to Egypt. Could they have foreseen all of this? No. But they continued to trust the One who had called them. Without question, God had found two hearts He could trust "in the fullness of time."

But in order to have a kinsman redeemer, you must have a widow. Death is always the pivotal point in activating the Law of the *Go'el*.

Mary was not the widow, but all of creation was. We, all believers, Jew or Gentile, are the widow. In fact, all of mankind since Adam were and are part of the widow. In the Law of the Kinsman Redeemer, the widow always had a choice to make as to whether or not she would be redeemed. Please hear me clearly, it is eternally the heart of the Father for all to come into covenant with Him, to be redeemed, and brought into His inheritance. But it continues to be a free choice. Our choice to be either a bride or a widow.

Adam had no brother in the flesh to redeem his widow when he brought death into creation. Adam was fashioned from clay and the Holy Spirit breathed life into his body. There had to be a relative in the flesh of the same blood line to qualify as a kinsman redeemer. In the womb the baby's blood never mixes with the mother's blood. To be the kinsman redeemer for Adam's widow, Jesus had to be from the same pure bloodline as Adam. Born 4000 years later, both Adam and Jesus had the same Father. Jesus became flesh as Adam's brother to qualify as the near kinsman to buy back and redeem all of creation.

"In the beginning was the Word, and the Word was with God, and the Word was God....And the Word became flesh and dwelt among us and we beheld His glory, the glory as of the only begotten of the Father, full of grace and truth." (John 1:1&14)

"Then I saw a strong angel proclaiming with a loud voice, "Who is worthy, suitable or qualified (*G514, Strongs*) to open the scroll and to loose its seals?" and no one in heaven or on the earth or under the earth was able to open the scroll, or to look at it. So I wept much, because no one was found worthy to open and read the scroll, or to look at it.
But one of the Elders said to me, "Do not weep. Behold, the Lion of the Tribe of Judah, the root of David, has prevailed to open the scroll and to loose its seven seals."
And I looked and behold, in the midst of the throne and of the four living creatures, and in the midst of the elders, stood a Lamb as though it had been slain….
And they sang a new song, saying:
"You are worthy to take the scroll, and to open its seals;
For you were slain, and by your blood have redeemed, purchased (*G59, Strongs*) us to God out of every tribe and tongue and people and nation." (Rev. 5:2-6)

The stories of these five matriarchs of our faith found in the first chapter of Matthew are filled with hope from hopeless situations; justice from unjust acts; life from barrenness; destiny and dignity instead of shame; covering and protection when exposed and uncovered; freedom out of bondage and death. These are the promises of the *Go'el*, the Kinsman Redeemer, as He gives beauty for ashes, the oil of joy for mourning and the garment of praise for the spirit of heaviness. The pure blood line of Jesus, the promised Messiah, our Kinsman Redeemer.

But Why Bethlehem?

Jehovah had spent four thousand years preparing, creating, and setting the stage for this moment. It is totally amazing to see how it all came together in a tiny little hamlet called Bethlehem.

Judah's Tribe came from the *Go'el* Redemption Law and was known as the *Go'el* Tribe. 1 Chron. 2:51 tells us Salmon, also found as Salma, was the father of Bethlehem and married Rahab. It was in Bethlehem, in the territory of Judah, where Boaz married Ruth and Bethlehem became known as the *Go'el* City. King David and Joseph, earthly father of Jesus were both from Bethlehem.

Bethlehem was known for it's delicious bread. How fitting that in the house of bread the Bread of Life was born.

Again, why Bethlehem?

Not only was this the *Go'el* City in the land of the *Go'el* Tribe. Also Bethlehem was the place where the sacrificial lambs were born. To qualify as a Passover lamb, the lamb had to be born in Bethlehem. Even so with the Lamb of God who takes away the sins of the world.

Have you ever wondered, as we retell the story of the birth of Jesus, why there seems to be one detail that has been overlooked? They could not find room in the inn so they went out back to the barn? It appears in our retelling that this was an "Oops" on behalf of Jehovah. But this was no oversight; it was a very intentional move on behalf of Jehovah. He had prepared a strategic, ceremonially clean place for Mary to give birth to Jesus.

The field where the angels appeared was at Migdal Eder, the Tower of the Flock just outside Bethlehem on the road to Jerusalem. The lambs born to this flock would be offered as sacrifices in the temple for the cleansing of sin. The shepherds who kept this flock were specifically trained by the rabbis. It was their job to make sure each lamb exactly fulfilled the specifications for the temple. None could be hurt, damaged or blemished. They were under strict rabbinical oversight to maintain a ceremonially clean stable as a birthing place.

These shepherds customarily kept their flocks outdoors twenty-four hours a day every day of the year, except when the ewes were brought into the birthing cave to deliver their lambs. It was in this cave where the Passover Lamb of God was to be born.

There was no need for the angels to give these shepherds directions to the birthplace. When the angel said the sign would be a manger, they knew he could only mean their manger. They hurriedly ran to the birthing cave to examine this new lamb, found to be without spot or blemish. As they left, they proclaimed to all what the angel had told them, "The Savior, who was their *Go'el* had been born!"

Why Bethlehem? Of course, Bethlehem! The house of bread, the city of the *Go'el,* and the birthplace of the Passover lamb. No other place on earth could have qualified except Bethlehem. In the fullness of time.

Chapter Six
A Closer Look at Weddings

Weddings are awe-inspiring pictures of covenant. Who isn't moved in their heart when they see the bride walk down the aisle in white or the look on the groom's face as he eagerly awaits his beloved at the altar? Jehovah has spent six thousand years painting pictures and images of covenant so that we would "get it." Each time a couple vows "til death do us part," covenant is again released into the earth.

As the mother of three daughters, I love weddings. From the initial proposal to the last bite of cake, I love the entire experience. I think my husband Billy Joe performs the best wedding ceremony I've heard (no prejudice here). One portion he always mentions is the difference between a covenant and a contract. As I began to look closely at wedding traditions, I discovered most are actually rooted in the covenant ceremony. Throughout the Bible, particularly in the context of the kinsman redeemer, there are two re-occurring themes—weddings and covenants. In fact, a closer look reveals they are one and the same. All of these are but a picture of the great Covenant with our Kinsman Redeemer.

American Wedding Customs and Traditions

Wedding traditions are found in all cultures. Some common traditions are the ring, the language of the ceremony, and the celebration meal.

Did he ask her yet? Has he popped the question? Clearly it is the groom who initiates the covenant by inviting her to be his bride.

A recent TV commercial features many different people sharing the news, "She said yes!" That, too, is a reflection of covenant. While he initiates, she makes the choice to say yes. Isn't that true in our relationship with Jesus? He calls, but we always have the choice to say "Yes."

By entering first at the ceremony, the groom assumes the greatest responsibility in the relationship, the responsibility for protection, provision, and spiritual leadership. He is laying the foundation for the marriage and his best man is the witness to the ceremony. By signing the license, the best man is legally documenting the wedding. In a covenant, there must always be a witness.

As the bride enters she walks between the two families recognizing that the two families are becoming one family in this union. Following the ceremony, the new couple also walks out between the two families. These two families represent the sacrifices made in order to bring the bride and groom to this point in their lives, a picture of the covenanting partners walking between the sacrifices.

At a wedding there are no uninvolved spectators, there are only covenant participants. Most family members do not realize they have become spiritual witnesses to this covenant and are responsible to hold them accountable for the vows made at this altar. As participants, we should always pray for the strength and commitment of the couple to be able to uphold the vows being made that day.

The exchange of wedding rings and the words "Until death do us part" are also a legal portion of the ceremony. At this point they are legally bound to each other before the Lord and the witnesses. The moment the husband places the ring on her finger she belongs to him alone. This ring is the outward sign to the world that they are in covenant with each other, they are becoming one. For anyone to try to divide the two would entail the fury of the other.

Remember, Jehovah first created the wedding band of covenant when He declared before eternity: "I set my bow in the cloud, and it shall be for the sign of the covenant between me and the earth." (Genesis 9:13)

The rainbow is a complete circle when seen from the sky above it. As this rainbow surrounds His throne, He is always reminded that we are His bride; He is eternally in covenant with us and longs for the day when we are one with Him at the Wedding Feast of the Lamb.

After the ceremony, comes the feast. We enjoy watching the bride and groom feed each other bites of wedding cake and give each other a sip of wine or punch. How many of us realize that this is their first communion, the sign of what is mine is yours and what is yours is mine? In my younger days before I understood covenant, I thought this was a strange custom. But it marks the beginning of the celebration of the wedding feast, the two becoming one. As they feed each other cake they are actually saying "All that I have in the earth is now yours." referring back to the Abrahamic covenant. The vows have been made at the altar and now the feast begins. Following a meal, dancing, and celebration, the bride and groom leave for their honeymoon. Intimacy always follows covenant.

Jewish Wedding Customs

One of the most beautiful pictures we have in the earth of covenant is the Jewish Wedding Ceremony. I am not Jewish and I'm sure I don't really know the fullness of all of the parts of this lovely, joyous celebration, but over the years I have been captivated by the beauty and the holiness found here. Each time I read more about it, my heart is stirred by the love that the Father and the Bridegroom has for us as individuals. How He longs to make covenant individually with each of us. How He looks at us with love and yearns for us to know His love, His devotion, His passion for us.

I have only witnessed one Jewish wedding from afar so therefore, I am not an expert on Jewish weddings, but as I have researched, I have been astounded at the intricate parts that make the whole of a

Jewish wedding. There is much symbolism and revelation of covenant in each part and it is easily seen how each portion mirrors one of the seven feasts of the Lord which also point to the wedding feast of our Kinsman Redeemer.

Although not all Jewish weddings still include each of these elements today, the beauty of our loving heavenly Father is very evident in each portion, insuring His bride is well cared for and secure. This ceremony paints a beautiful picture of how precious you are to the Father and His Son.

The Betrothal and The *Mohar* - the Bride Price. In ancient Hebrew times the father and the son would choose a bride, go to her home and discuss the marriage with the bride's family. After coming to an agreement, making sure the groom had the resources to fulfill his vows of commitment to care for her, protect her, and provide for her, a written covenant document was signed. It was called a Ketubah. At this point the choice had been made and the bridegroom had made his vows of commitment to the bride and her family. They also agreed on a mohar, or bride price. This was paid to the family of the bride, but ultimately belonged to the bride.

He then offered the bride a valuable gift, usually a ring. If she accepted this gift, then the betrothal was sealed. At this point the couple was bound to each other legally and to separate would require a divorce. Remember that Mary and Joseph were betrothed to each other.

After the arrangements were made, the father and son would go back to the father's house and the son would prepare a home for his bride. Only when the father was convinced the preparations were finished would he release his son to go and get his bride. She was to be preparing for her wedding, so that when she heard the announcement, "The bridegroom is coming!" she could quickly be ready to meet him for their wedding. Her father would also be ready and the wedding ceremony would take place immediately, followed by a feast lasting for seven days.

Mary and Joseph were betrothed but had not had their wedding ceremony. These customs are still practiced in some Middle Eastern cultures today.

Cultures have shifted, communication and travel have speeded up causing the timeline of some of these beautiful proceedings to be altered. For instance, in the past the betrothal occurred weeks, months, or even a year prior to the wedding. Today, in many Orthodox ceremonies, both the betrothal and wedding ceremony are commonly held on the same day. Whether the betrothal occurs prior to or on the day of the wedding, it still carries the same weighty importance legally and spiritually. If the betrothal has not occurred prior to the wedding, the ceremony will be divided into two parts: the betrothal which includes the reading of the *Ketubah* and the giving of the ring. When the bride accepts the ring, the betrothal portion of the wedding is considered done. The reading of the *Ketubah* gives a little break and then the official wedding ceremony begins.

The *Ketubah*, the written Marriage Covenant. If the betrothal has not occurred prior to the wedding day, a small reception for the groom, called the groom's *Tisch*, or groom's table, is held before the ceremony where the signing of the *Ketubah* takes place. The *Ketubah* is a legal document defining the groom's responsibilities to provide his wife with food, shelter, and clothing, and also to be attentive to her emotional needs. It outlines his resources to show that he is fully capable of fulfilling his promises. Protecting the rights of a Jewish wife is so important that the marriage may not be solemnized until this covenant document is approved by the father of the bride, the father of the groom and the rabbi. Then it is signed by the groom and two witnesses. Traditional law holds that only adult Jewish males not related to the bride or groom by either blood or marriage may serve as witnesses.

The *Ketubah* has the standing of a legally binding agreement and is read aloud during the betrothal portion of the ceremony after the groom gives her the ring. This document of the covenant belongs solely to the bride as proof of her rights. Many times it is decorated with beautiful art work and kept in an honored place in the home as a reminder of their covenant and all that it entails.

I am astounded at how meticulously the Father has been planning His Son's wedding for 6000 years. What a powerful and compelling picture of Jesus, our bridegroom. He made His vows of commitment at Passover, cutting covenant with us. According to Jewish tradition, Jehovah gave His *Ketubah*, His betrothal document of Torah, to the nation of Israel on Mount Sinai which is celebrated as the Feast of *Shavuot*. As a fulfillment of this feast Jesus gave us the gift of the Holy Spirit to seal our betrothal.

Can you see the amazing *Ketubah* we have from our bridegroom? The entire Bible outlines all that He is and all that He will do for us as His bride. The witnesses? Hebrews 12 tells us that there is a great cloud of witnesses who are watching as His story unfolds in eternity.

Not only does this document contain all that He will do for us, His bride, it includes His assets. Our *Go'el* has more than enough resources to provide all that we need according to His riches in Glory.

The *Badeken*, the First Look. *Badeken* means "to cover" and during this portion of the ceremony the groom veils his bride. Although in most cultures it is customary for the groom and bride not to see each other on the day of their wedding, in some sects of Judaism the bride and groom may not see each other for the week prior to the wedding. Either way, they both fast on the day of their wedding. It's often an emotional moment when the bride and groom see each other for the first time a few minutes before the main ceremony begins. This is called the "first look" on their wedding day.

I love the explanation that the veil is a garment of modesty dating back to when Rebecca veiled herself prior to meeting Isaac. It symbolizes that the groom is marrying his bride for her inner beauty, her soul, and character, not just her physical beauty. At this special moment, the parents and rabbi bless them with the traditional Jewish blessing usually pronounced on Sabbath. As he places the veil over his beloved's face he is affirming to all those present, "She is set apart for me alone. I am assuming the responsibility to clothe her, protect her, and love her."

Can you imagine the "first look" of our bridegroom? Philippians tells us that we see through a glass darkly, then we shall see Him face to face. This will be our first look. The Song of Solomon is a lovely glimpse into the love of the bridegroom for His bride. He calls her altogether lovely and declares to her

"One glance of your eyes has captured my heart ... a raging flood cannot drown out my love for you" (Song of Sol. 8:6-7).

What security in Him to know that we have been set apart, made holy for Him alone. Our *Go'el* will not relent until He has all of our heart. He has covered us with His love and sealed us with His Holy Spirit until that day when He comes to claim us as His own. Can you hear Him calling? We are the fire in His eyes.

The *Chuppah* or Canopy. At every Jewish wedding the one essential is the *chuppah*, a tapestry or a *tallit* attached to the tops of four poles sometimes held by family or friends. It symbolizes the bridal chamber or new home being prepared and established by the bridegroom, the sign of covering and protection, the sign of Jehovah's covenant covering over both the bride and groom. His banner over us is His love. As we choose to step under His *chuppah* we are coming into His house, His kingdom, becoming His bride. Open on all sides as a symbol of hospitality, the new home will welcome all those who come.

The groom, along with his father and mother, enter first to show that he is the one initiating this covenant and has his father's approval. Entering with her parents, the bride stops midway down the aisle as her parents continue on. When they are in place, the groom leaves to greet and escort his bride under his *chuppah*. Stepping under the *chuppah* with her groom, she formally proclaims her choice to leave her father's house and become his wife, his covenant partner under his spiritual covering.

The Seven Circles. The custom of the bride circling the groom seven times is rich with symbolism. We remember that the Hebrew word for oath literally means "To seven one's self to another." As she circles her groom seven times she is saying "I will seven you. We are creating a new family through covenant and I am building a wall of covenant around our home." This is her oath of covenant, setting aside her marriage as holy to the Lord. This is her response to her husband's invitation to come into covenant. We always have a choice in covenant. Not only does our *Go'el* choose to come and marry us, we too have a choice to make. Our response toward Him is to say, "Yes, I will 'seven' you."

The *Kiddush* or the Betrothal. Under the *chuppah* there are two cups of wine. As the rabbi recites the blessing of sanctification and joy over the first cup, now they are betrothed to each other and shall have no other physical partners after they drink from this first cup.

Following this cup the marriage becomes official as the groom gives his bride a solid gold ring, declaring: "Behold, you are consecrated unto me with this ring according to the laws of Moses and Israel."

At this point the *Ketubah* is read to all who are present as a public proclamation of the groom's responsibility toward his beloved and the betrothal is complete.

The *Tallit* Wrap. Although this is not done in every wedding, it is one of the most intimate portions of the ceremony. Following the betrothal, the groom wraps the bride in his personal *tallit* and the rabbi blesses them with personal blessings. Just as Boaz covered Ruth with his *tallit*, the groom is honoring her commitment to him and is receiving her into his heart under his personal covenant with Jehovah. She is under his *tallit* of intimacy and he is publically proclaiming, "I will protect you, cover you, avenge you, and pay your debts. As one before the Lord we receive our full inheritance together."

A Closer Look at Weddings

The *Sheva Brachot,* Seven Blessings. The rabbi now recites the seven blessings over the second cup of wine. The theme of these blessings links the couple to their faith in God as creator of the world, as the giver of joy and love and as the ultimate redeemer of the Jewish people. It is this cup we will share with our Bridegroom at the Wedding Feast of the Lamb.

The Breaking of the Glass. Nothing says Jewish wedding like the sound of breaking glass and the shouts of "*Mazel Tov!*" "*L'Chaim!*" Following the second cup of wine, a glass is wrapped in a napkin, placed on the floor and the groom breaks the glass with his right foot and joy explodes in the room. The vows are complete and the celebration begins. Everyone present has just witnessed a solemn, holy occasion and now it is time to celebrate.

I never understood the custom of the breaking of the glass until recently. Tradition says the breaking of the glass is to remember the destruction of the temple and to identify the couple with the spiritual and national destiny of the Jewish people. A Jew, even at the moment of greatest rejoicing, is mindful of the Psalmist's injunction:

> "If I forget you, Jerusalem, let my right hand forget how to play the lyre. Let my tongue stick to the roof of my mouth. If I don't remember you, if I don't consider Jerusalem my highest joy." (Psalm 137:5-6, GW).

As the crushing of the glass sounds throughout the wedding venue, all hearts turn toward Jerusalem, remembering the God of Abraham, Isaac, and Jacob and lamenting for the rebuilding of the Temple.

Recently my pastor John Gowen, taught about the importance of the Temple in Jewish life. The Temple gave Israel an identity as a people, set apart as holy unto the Lord. The Tabernacle first and then the Temple was their point of contact, their connection to the God of Abraham, Isaac, and Jacob. This connection was continually being reaffirmed with the daily sacrifice and the yearly cycle of the seven feasts, always to be celebrated in Jerusalem.

I am a Gentile Christian living in the South, where Christian churches of numerous varieties fill my city. I have a choice as to which one I identify as my own. This is not so with the Jewish people. Under His covenant God chose only one city in all the earth in which to set His name and that city is Jerusalem.

The Temple represented their connection to the God of Abraham, the root of their identity. The Temple was the only acceptable place of worship where the sacrifices were made, their sin was forgiven, and covenant rituals performed. If there was no Temple, there was no concrete connection to Jehovah through sacrifice and offerings. The lament of Psalm 137:4, "How shall we sing the song of the Lord in a strange or foreign land?" still rings true today for the Jewish people. They continually remember and long for the Temple to be rebuilt as promised.

As grafted-in Gentile Christians, we understand the real temple is not the one that stood in Jerusalem but is the one not made with hands. Jesus is the temple that was destroyed and was raised up on the third day. His blood is the eternal sacrifice poured out on the eternal altar. He is our concrete connection with God. It is in Him that we live and move and have our being according to Acts 27.

But is Jerusalem still important? Is it meaningful to me as a grafted-in Gentile? Yes. Jerusalem is the city where Jesus was sacrificed as the Passover Lamb. Jerusalem is where the Messianic church was birthed and spread throughout the world. Our churches today came from that small group of Jewish believers in Jerusalem. And Jerusalem is the city to which our bridegroom will return to claim us as His bride. Jerusalem is the only city in the earth for which we are commanded to pray (See Psalm 122). In the book of Revelation, John says,

> "And I, John, saw the holy city, Jerusalem, coming down from heaven as a bride adorned for her husband" (Rev. 21:2).

If this city is still important to God, then it is important to me.

We look toward Jerusalem with expectancy and we pray for peace to be within her walls. The Temple Mount is the most contested tiny piece of real estate in the earth. There is an amazing rise of Messianic believers in Israel and other nations who are the cousins of the Messiah. As the Gentile body of Christ, we stand with this remnant of the true vine as one new man according to Ephesians, until the day His feet once again touch the Mountain of the Lord in Jerusalem.

The *Yichud*. As the party begins, the couple is escorted to a private *yichud* room to share some peaceful, private moments, signifying their new status of living together as husband and wife. Breaking their wedding day fast, they enjoy a light meal of bread and wine. This is an important lesson for marriage. The couple should never allow the hustle and bustle of life to completely engulf them; they must always find private time for each other. It is also a time when the bride and groom customarily exchange gifts.

We too must stop amid the clatter of everyday life and pull away to our *yichud* room, better known to us as our prayer closet, our secret place. Most of us go to our prayer closet, not necessarily to spend time with Him there, but to petition Him for our urgent needs. Our *Go'el* longs for us to come away with Him into that quiet place, to share an intimate moment of communion with Him.

When we think of communion, we think bread and wine, which, yes, is an intricate part of our time with Him. But the word communion means so much more. It literally means to share intimate thoughts and feelings with one another, especially on a spiritual level. Looking deeper at Psalm 91 we hear His call of covenant. The word "dwell" actually means to marry or remain. The word "wing" is His *tallit*, His little tent, our secret place of His covenant protection. In the Song of Solomon, the bridegroom continually calls us to come away. In those intimate moments we can petition, not as a widow begging, but as His cherished bride, His covenant partner.

The *Seudah*, the Festive Meal. It is a *mitzvah* (a command or good deed) for guests to bring simcha (joy) to the bride and groom on their wedding day. In other words, they are commanded to celebrate! There is dancing and feasting to celebrate this newly created family.

This celebrating continues for seven days, as others bring meals or gifts to the couple, joining in with their joy and releasing blessings to this new family.

The Word tells us all of heaven celebrates when one lost soul comes into the kingdom. Personally, I have seen joy as optional, but in reality, we are commanded to have joy and to celebrate. I don't know about you, but I like that. Sometimes in our misunderstanding of trying to describe His holiness, we reflect on words like somber, solemn, or restrained. But at this high, holy moment of marriage we are commanded to bring joy and to celebrate. There is nothing more delightful than hearing a little one giggle. To hear that bubbling laughter causes us to bubble up too, or at least to smile. We are commanded to be like little children in our walk with the Lord. Now putting those two thoughts together, what if as we worshiped, we shared our intimate times with Him in laughter, giggles, and great joy! A novelty? I hope not.

We had a dear friend who was preaching at a little country church and he described the congregation this way. "They looked like they had been to a dill pickle sucking contest." A funny but a sad commentary on some of our corporate times of worship. I believe it could be a *mitzvah* (good deed) to bring *simcha* (joy) into our corporate times of fellowship and our private times with our *Go'el*. After all it's a command!

Chapter Seven
The Covenant Feasts of the Kinsman Redeemer

As we look at God's plan for the seven Feasts, especially in light of the Jewish wedding feast, each intricate detail gives greater insight into His word, His love and His plan for our destiny. Celebrating these Feasts continues to unveil our eyes to see our Messiah Jesus as He walked out the fullness of covenant in the earth.

This is my very simplified view of the Feasts. I have only scratched the surface of their meaning. There are others with years of observing and studying who would have much more insight than I do and may find my views to be very shallow. As a Gentile believer I have attempted to appreciate and observe God's commanded times and seasons as best I could in my limited understanding, and because of this study my walk with the Lord has grown deeper, richer, and more liberating in many areas of my life.

All of the feasts encompass the covenant and portray the *Go'el,* the Kinsman Redeemer, coming to redeem us, pay our debts, marry us, and restore our lost inheritance we enjoyed in the garden. The description of the seven Feasts are pictures of what the covenant would look like in the earth, a dress rehearsal of the Wedding Feast of the Lamb. The Passover out of Egypt was the beginning of the redemption of the widow, Israel.

The Feast of Passover and Unleavened Bread

Passover, Unleavened Bread and First Fruits are the first of the spring feasts on God's calendar. Passover is one night only to commemorate the night Jehovah "passed over" the homes with the blood of the lamb on their doorposts. The same night also begins the seven days of Unleavened Bread to remember that Jehovah commanded the Israelites to leave Egypt in such a hurry there was no time for their bread to rise. The day following Passover was a Sabbath to be followed by First Fruits celebration on the third day. Today many people simply call the entire seven days Passover.

In preparation for the Feast of Unleavened Bread the Israelites were told to get all of the yeast out of their house. This yeast represents the sin in our lives and we are told to examine and cleanse our homes of the yeast, just as a reminder to examine and cleanse our lives of sin. The unleavened bread is a picture of Jesus' holiness and sinless life. This bread reminds us that He was pure, without sin, an unblemished lamb.

The unleavened bread, used at the Passover meal, was prepared in a special way. Prior to baking, it was stripped and pierced to prevent it from rising at all. When Jesus held up this bread, He declared "this is my body." Truly it was a picture of what was to come as foretold in Isaiah.

> "But He was wounded for our transgressions, bruised for our iniquities; the chastisement for our peace was upon Him, and by His stripes we are healed." (Isaiah 53:5)

The Feast of First Fruits was celebrated the third day following Passover. This feast commemorated the first portion of their barley harvest. They were to bring the first sheaf of the harvest to the priest and he would present it as a wave offering, sanctifying the entire harvest to come. The first fruits sanctified the whole. Jesus rose from the dead on the morning of First Fruits. He was the first fruit of resurrection, sanctifying the whole, the resurrection of the redeemed.

Passover

Of all the Feasts we celebrate, there is none more poignant than Passover. It was at His last Passover that Jesus began the journey of the blood path of the covenant ceremony. During His last night with His friends as His witnesses, the bridegroom took the oath of betrothal to deliver His bride.

"In that day I will make a covenant with them
I will betroth you to Me forever;
Yes, I will betroth you to Me
In righteousness and justice; in lovingkindness and mercy;
I will betroth you to Me in faithfulness,
Then I will say ..."You are My people!"
And they shall say, "You are my God!"
(Hosea 2:18-23 the Voice)
"All we like sheep have gone astray; we have turned every one to his own way. And the Lord has laid on Him the iniquity of us all." (Isaiah 53:6)
"And on the night He was betrayed, He took the cup and blessed it and said, "this is my blood of the new covenant." (1 Corinthians 11:25)

With eagerness yet dread of what lay before Him, Jesus said to His friends, "Let's go up to Jerusalem for Passover." When He spoke these words to His disciples did they sense the bittersweet joy mixed with sorrow in His voice as He looked up to the hills of the city? Joy at what lay before Him, knowing His obedience would please His Father; joy of paying the *go'el* price to claim His bride; yet sorrow and dread of the suffering He must endure as the ultimate Passover Lamb.

As a young boy in Nazareth, Jesus had studied the Messianic prophecies and knew them well. He had walked through the script of Passover for thirty-two years. Familiar with the Roman cross, He knew the torture, pain, and agony that awaited Him in Jerusalem. He even spoke of it in those last hours at the Passover meal with His friends. But He also said to them, "I have longed to celebrate this Passover with you."

He had been born for this day.

Five days before the Seder Feast of Passover, Jesus rode into Jerusalem on a donkey. The shouts of Hosanna rang out in the streets of the city, deafening the bleating of the sacrificial lambs being brought into the city along the same path that very day.

During these five days, just as the lambs were examined by the chief priest, so was the Lamb of God examined and questioned by the same chief priest.

In looking past the horror of the cross, in His last conversation with His friends, Jesus mentioned "joy" seven times. Paul tells us in Hebrews it was for this joy that He endured the cross -- the joy of seeing His Father's face again, the joy of hearing "Well done, my good and faithful servant," and the joy of redeeming you, His bride.

For almost two thousand years this appointed time had been prophesied, discussed, debated, and rehearsed at Passover. In fact, since the fall in the Garden of Eden, all of creation had longed for the curse to be broken. This Passover would mark the beginning of the biggest shift in history: the shift from the old to the new, the covenant of redemption fulfilled. We would now see the old in the revelation of the new, the new covenant.

Knowing this Seder meal would be their last meal together, He invited the disciples to sit and He washed their feet, including the feet of Judas.

> "Jesus, knowing that the Father had given all things into His hands, and that He had come from God and was going to God, rose from supper and laid aside His garments, took a towel and girded Himself. After that, He poured water into a basin and began to wash the disciples' feet, and to wipe them with the towel with which He was girded." (John 13:3-5)

Yes, this Passover night would be different from all of the ones celebrated for two thousand years. Jesus, ever the servant-king, secure in who He was and what He had come to do, took a towel, and washed their feet.

This Passover night Jesus would taste the salty water and bitter herbs as a stark reminder of the bitter tears of slavery that held His bride captive. As one by one the defeat of the Egyptian gods was recounted during this Seder meal, He knew that one by one He would face these lesser demonic enemies until He would finally come face to face with the prince of darkness himself. Yet even in understanding all of this, He knew He had come to earth for one purpose: to pay the ultimate bride price to redeem His creation, His Other. He had created her and now He would buy her back.

Rising at the head of the table, all eyes were upon Him as He stood before the entire universe declaring His vows of covenant, His vows as our *Go'el*, our Kinsman Redeemer. Every jot and tittle in the Torah, He would now fulfill.

Heaven reverberated as the Son of God raised the first of the four cups of Passover, the cup of Sanctification and declared, "I will bring you out ..."

Jehovah had said to Moses, "I will bring you out of Egypt as a nation." Jacob took His family into Egypt as a small clan, hungry, poor, and needy, but Jehovah had brought them out as a great and wealthy nation of twelve tribes. As Jesus drank this cup, He vowed to bring us out of our Egypt, out of our desperate circumstances, out of the spirit of poverty, and into His Kingdom, into our inheritance as His bride.

Next came the second cup, the cup of Deliverance. Holding it high He proclaimed, "I will deliver you...."

At the first Passover, Jehovah proclaimed, "I will deliver you from the slavery of Egypt by my strong right arm." Now Jesus was proclaiming, "I will deliver you from the slavery of sin and shame by my strong right arm."

Shame was one of the first demonic spirits to attack Adam and Eve causing them to cover themselves with a fig leaf. Shame lands deep in our spirit and soul, urging us to hide, to look for a fig leaf. As one of the deepest wounds, it propels us into self-rejection and self-loathing. This pierces the Father's heart even deeper than the spear that would pierce His Son's side. He declares to us in myriads of ways, "I love you. I created you. You are mine." But this self-loathing, lying spirit whispers deeply to us, "Even God does not know who you really are. If God actually knew, He would spit you out!" This despicable lie of our enemy pushes us to hide even deeper in loneliness and self-hate, and to refuse to believe the truth. It not only takes forgiveness to break the bondage of slavery, but it also takes the strong right arm of deliverance from Lord *Sabaoth*, the commander of the angel armies, to set us free.

Jesus understood "identity" was the issue allowing shame to have an entry into our heart and soul. To feel uncovered drives us toward shame. When He laid aside His glory to come to earth, Jesus was uncovered, but shame could not enter because He knew who He was, He knew why He came and He knew where He was going. Jesus had no identity issues. As we receive the forgiveness and deliverance at the cross, we are delivered out of the shame of this demonic lie to grasp the truth of who we are, where we came from, and where we are going. From this foundational revelation, the demonic whispering is replaced with soothing words of love, peace, and acceptance. Our Kinsman Redeemer not only delivers us from the curse of shame, but also gives us our identity as His own, covering us with His covenant so that we are hidden in Him.

On each Seder table there are three loaves of unleavened bread stacked within a napkin. The center piece of bread is called the *afikomen*, a Greek word meaning, "He who is coming." Just as Jesus' body would be beaten, pierced, and striped from a whip, this bread is striped and pierced as it is baked. Earlier in the Seder this center piece of bread is broken, wrapped in a napkin, and hidden, just as His body would be broken, wrapped in linen, and hidden in a tomb for three days. Following the cup of Deliverance, the children are sent to find this mysterious piece of bread.

As He lifted this bread high, He blessed it, saying, "This is my body given for you." Until now this Passover had appeared to be the same as had been celebrated for two thousand years. However, with these words Jesus shifted from the traditional *Haggadah* or Passover script into the profound revelation of Himself as the Passover Lamb. At this Passover, the "He who is coming!" had come. Passover could never be the same.

After passing around the bread, He folded the napkin and placed it to the side. Although this napkin had been folded in the same manner for two thousand years, later the disciples would realize the significance of this act. Earlier we noted that it was customary for the tallit of the person to be wrapped around His head in preparation for burial. Each man folded His *tallit* in His own unique way and Jesus was no different. The disciples had seen exactly how He had folded His *tallit* for three years. Advancing toward resurrection day, when Peter and John entered the empty tomb, they noted that the napkin or *tallit* was not with the other linen grave cloths. It was folded precisely as Jesus had folded it and laid it to the side. He had left them this sign, recognizable from the Passover meal.

Now taking the third cup, the cup of Redemption, He announced "I will redeem you (buy you back) by my outstretched arm, my power." Continuing, "This is my blood of the new covenant which is poured out for many for the forgiveness of sin." He was professing His intent to make the supreme sacrifice of His holy blood to cut a new covenant in the earth. What had taken place before the creation of time would now be enacted in the earth. Jesus Christ, slain from the foundation of the earth.

The time had come.

The fourth cup, the cup of Restoration, was not taken that night. Jesus will not drink of this cup until He drinks it with us in His restored Kingdom. We will celebrate this cup at our wedding feast when creation is fully restored, clothed in glory and light so beautifully described in John's book of Revelation.

During the meal that night, Jesus no longer spoke to His disciples in parables, but as dear friends, giving them His last instructions. Then He prayed,

> "Father my time has come. Glorify your son and I will bring you great glory because you have given me total authority over humanity....I have glorified you on earth and fulfilled the mission you set before me. (John 17:1-4, NIV)

Following this prayer they went out into the garden. Although there are four traditional cups at Passover, this night there was a fifth cup, the one offered and accepted in the Garden of Gethsemane: the cup of God's wrath against the nations, the cup from which He would drink as the disciples slept. Jeremiah states,

> "This is a Message that the God of Israel gave me: 'Take this cup filled with the wine of my wrath that I'm handing to you'" (Jeremiah 25:15 MSG).

Jesus sweat drops of blood as He drank this cup in agony for the nations. Before His ascension Jesus told the believers, "Go and disciple the nations." This last cup in the garden prepared the way for the nations to be transformed and brought into His Kingdom.

Recently during a time with our friends, Kay and Tom Schlueter, Tom shared a stirring revelation with us. As Jesus prayed to His Father in the garden there was an amazing exchange between them. Many times Jesus went early to communicate with His Father, but most of these times He went alone. This evening was different. On this Passover night He invited the three disciples closest to Him to come along and watch. For what were they watching? The soldiers? Judas? I had actually never thought about it until Tom mentioned it to us.

As John tells us, they were tired and all fell asleep. Jesus came back to them, possibly a little disappointed, to admonish them again to watch. What was it He wanted them to see?

The Covenant Feasts of the Kinsman Redeemer

Could He have been asking them to watch something that was eternal? Could He have been giving them a first-hand demonstration of how to communicate with the Father? What an opportunity to have witnessed the intimacy of the Father and His beloved Son. Yet, they slept as this touching moment took place. They could have witnessed the Father's hand as He reached down to encourage, comfort and strengthen His Son. As the drops of bloody sweat poured down His face, they could have seen the gentleness of the angels as they ministered to Jesus in His most vulnerable moments on earth. They could have observed the exchange of Father and Son at the pinnacle of shared agony: the very moment when He resolved in His heart to obey and drink this bitter cup.

Would their perception of prayer have been enriched? Could they have, by the sheer intensity of the moment, had a deeper comprehension of the magnitude of His sacrifice? We don't know. We do know they were tired and in their human weakness they slept. Would I have slept too? Sadly, probably so.

When the soldiers came for Him in the garden, Judas betrayed Him with a kiss and the sacrifice of covenant began. A crown of thorns was placed on His head along with the mockery of a trial. He was spit upon, beaten, judged, and condemned by the religious establishment of the day. And it started with a kiss.

While the Roman soldiers commenced the crucifixion, another drama was being played out at the temple. Brought to the altar at 9:00 am, the priest put the Passover lamb on display for all to see the purity of this unblemished lamb. On a hill outside the city gates Jesus, our Passover Lamb was lifted on the cross for all to see His sacrifice. For the next six hours, He walked the blood path of Abraham's covenant as He cut a new covenant with all of creation.

Cutting covenant is not a pretty sight. It is brutal. It is bloody. But it is holy.

As I was pondering the crucifixion one morning I had a vision of Lord *Sabaoth*, in full battle array stepping down from His brilliant white war steed and standing at attention, armed, ready, and fully able to defeat the foes of hell and the grave. I watched as this mighty warrior king regally removed His helmet releasing it to His enemy nearby. Instead of drawing His sword, He bowed His head. As a crown of thorns pierced His scalp drops of blood began to trickle down His strong, solemn face. At that moment I realized the price of my helmet of salvation spoken of in Ephesians. Rather than a crown of glory and light He wore the crown of thorns. I wept as I realized how lightly I take each portion of my spiritual armor. The price was paid in blood.

Next I saw Him take off and lay aside His royal robe, His robe of authority. He was stripped, no longer covered, so I could have the privilege and honor of being covered by His covenant robe, His *tallit*. As He handed over all of His weapons, the demonic forces cheered and the angelic host of heaven stood at attention awaiting the signal to attack. A signal which never came.

The sound of the cat-o'-nine tails lash reverberated in my ears. I tried to stop the noise and chaos, the horror of what I was witnessing, but the cruelty continued. The skin on His back was torn into bloody shreds, yet He spoke not a word. Our Kinsman Redeemer would wait until the cross to speak His last profound words, releasing forgiveness to His executioners. As the blood ran down His back to His legs and feet, Isaiah's prophecy was fulfilled: by His stripes we are healed.

This was the blood path He must walk for my redemption. This is the price of covenant keeping. As I gazed upon this warrior King, beaten, bloodied, and in such agony, the Lord's voice whispered: Behold, your Covenant Keeper.

No. Cutting covenant is not a pretty sight. It is brutal. It is bloody. But it is ever so holy.

The hand of the Lord is mentioned 1273 times in the Bible. His hand is terrible, strong, mighty, and gentle. By His hand He does wonders, saves, delivers, creates, and heals. Yet again Isaiah's prophecy was fulfilled as He willingly allowed the Roman soldiers to engrave your name on the palm of His hand with a nine-inch spike. (Isaiah 49).

The piercing of His beautiful feet was the price paid for us to leap, to dance, and to walk in His paths of righteousness and peace.

"How beautiful upon the mountains are the feet of those who bring us the gospel of peace" (Isaiah 52:7).

Again, Father, forgive us when we take all that He did for us for granted.

At three in the afternoon, the lamb at the temple was sacrificed by cutting its throat. As the blood ran down the sides of the altar, the priest shouted, "It is finished! The debt has been paid."

Simultaneously, outside of the city high on the hill of Golgotha, the voice of the Lamb of God rang out across eternity: "It is finished! The debt has been paid!"

When Jesus shouted "It is finished!" the Hebrew word is *"ASAH"* which means to complete, to create, to bring to perfection, to make war, and to avenge. In essence, Jesus, the Lion of Judah, roared triumphantly *"ASAH!* Accomplished! The debt is paid in full. I have avenged and made war. I have brought her to perfection. Come forth new creation!" The power of the cross is wrapped up in one word, *"ASAH!"* Our debt for sin has been paid; we can now walk out the rest of life as a new creation engraved on the palm of His hand.

As blood and water flowed from His side, He gave birth to this new creation, His bride, making her pure and spotless, giving her new life and victory over her arch enemy, the prince of darkness, Lucifer. At this moment the Bridegroom flung His *tallit* over all creation, covering her once again with His glory, once again in intimacy. This was the "*Tallit* wrap" of the ages. She was His because He created her and now she was His because He had paid the full bride price to buy her back. *ASAH!*

Just as in Passover tradition the bread was wrapped in a linen napkin and hidden away, so was the Bread of Life taken from the cross, wrapped in linen cloths, and buried in a rich man's tomb with a napkin, His *tallit*, placed over His face. The Passover Feast had been fulfilled.

Did this fulfillment end the celebration of Passover and the Feast of Unleavened Bread? No. Now the old was fulfilled so that all of the benefits have become accessible not only to Abraham's descendants, but to all nations. As with all covenants, we are instructed to remember and celebrate them on a regular basis. As we celebrate Passover, we, too, can shout, "*Asah*! come forth new creation!" We are reminded again of His triumph over our enemies and we witness the fullness of God's Kingdom coming in the earth.

Gathering as families, our eyes should now be opened to see how this feast is the embodiment of our salvation and to see how costly was the price paid for our freedom. Rather than the yearly sacrifice of the Passover lamb, our celebration points to the eternal sacrifice of Jesus, the Lamb of God. It increases our revelation of how Jesus, the Son of Man, came as our Kinsman Redeemer, fulfilling every detail of the Law of the *Go'el*.

During the Seder meal of Passover, we not only see the strong arm of deliverance from Egyptian slavery, we recognize the penalty and sacrifice for our liberation from the slavery of sin and shame. We not only commemorate the defeat of the ten gods of Egypt by the plagues, but it is a foretaste of the triumphant defeat of God's ancient enemy, Satan. The blood of goats and lambs would no longer cover the doorpost of a wooden house for one more year, the blood of Jesus would cover the entire household of creation for all eternity.

As He awakened from the dead on the Feast of First Fruits as the First Fruits of resurrection did He grasp His side? Just as Eve came from Adam's side, the wound in His side could only mean one thing: His bride was in the earth. His bride had come forth out of His side. The whole earth shook in celebration as the Kinsman Redeemer triumphantly stepped out of the tomb, defeating death, hell, and the grave. The great *Go'el* had come to claim His bride, His Other. No longer a captive, her bondage was broken and her full inheritance returned.

It is interesting that the first person to see Him was Mary, a woman redeemed from the bondage of demons. Because of her deep gratitude and love for Him, she had anointed Him with precious ointment, preparing Him for burial. Did she know she was the first fruit of many to come, a beautiful picture of the bride of Christ? Probably not, but He knew. *ASAH!*

Most Gentile believers do not celebrate Passover. We celebrate the crucifixion and the resurrection, but we miss the majesty, the richness, the fullness, and the profound intricacies of the sacrifice of our Kinsman Redeemer found in the Feast of Passover, Unleavened Bread, and First Fruits. We miss a portion of truth of the New Covenant that has been tucked into and hidden in the Old Covenant for centuries. In the New Testament, we are told:

> "Therefore purge out the old leaven, that you may be a new lump, since you truly are unleavened. For indeed, Messiah (Christ), our Passover, was sacrificed for us. Therefore, let us keep the feast, not with old leaven, nor with the leaven of malice and wickedness, but with the unleavened bread of sincerity and truth."(I Corinthians 5:7-8)

Observing the Seder meal of Passover and Unleavened Bread add to the glorious celebration of First Fruits of Resurrection Day because we grasp the significance of how the Old Covenant always pointed to the New Covenant, the precious Lamb of God, slain from the foundation of the world. On that Passover night so long ago, our *Go'el*, our Kinsman Redeemer, covered us with His *tallit* as He cut the oath of blood covenant with His Beloved Bride.

Jesus. The Passover Lamb. The Covenant Keeper. Our *Go'el*.

Shavuot/Pentecost

The Feast of *Shavuot* or Pentecost followed fifty days after First Fruits commemorating the giving of Torah on Mount Sinai. During this feast Jehovah *Elohim* swore eternal devotion to the Israelites, His Oath of Betrothal, giving them Torah and in turn, they promised everlasting loyalty to Him. The two necessary elements mentioned in the Jewish wedding tradition were present: The signing of the *Ketubah* or legal document and the giving and receiving of a valuable gift to seal the agreement. Torah was given to the Jewish nation as an outline for a wise and understanding way of life. It also described the goodness and resources of Jehovah *Elohim* and His promise to protect, provide, and keep them. Just as the wedding *Ketubah* is kept in an honored place in a Jewish home, so Jehovah's *Ketubah* was kept in the Tabernacle in a golden box called the Ark of the Covenant. Knowing that the Israelites could never keep the high standard of holiness required by this Law, He instructed them to place this golden box under the Mercy Seat where the blood of the Lamb would be sprinkled. His heart of love would always make a way for mercy to cover the Law.

When celebrating *Shavuot*, it is traditional to stay up all night reading, studying, and celebrating Torah, His Word. After Jesus had ascended into heaven following His resurrection, His disciples gathered together in an upper room in Jerusalem to celebrate this feast. Suddenly the Living Torah, the Holy Spirit, appeared in power with wind and fire. Jehovah *Elohim* was writing His Torah on hearts just as Isaiah and Jeremiah said He would, changing hearts to flesh rather than stone, empowering and sealing us with the gift of Himself, the Holy Spirit, guaranteeing our inheritance. This valuable gift sealed the Betrothal with our Kinsman Redeemer. From that day forward the Kingdom of God exploded in the earth, reaching outside of the Jewish boundaries, bringing the Gentiles into this amazing covenant of redemption and freedom. The Holy Spirit was creating the new bride, the "One New Man" of Ephesians. *ASAH!* The New has come.

The Fall Feasts: Trumpets, *Yom Kippur*/Day of Atonement and *Sukkot*/Tabernacles

The fall feasts are next on God's calendar. From my understanding these feasts are yet to be fulfilled by our Kinsman Redeemer. We look to these feasts in anticipation of what is to come.

Rosh Hashanah, which means "Head of the Year," marks the beginning of the Jewish civil calendar and Gentiles usually call this the Jewish New Year. The Feast of Trumpets is on the same day when the shofar—rams horn—is sounded to prepare our hearts for the High Holy Day of Atonement, Yom Kippur, to follow ten days later. During these ten days we are not only to marvel at the splendor and majesty of our Great King, but also to examine our own hearts to make ourselves ready for this day of repentance. As believers we understand the Blood of Jesus has taken away our sin, but it is always good to stop, take inventory of our lives and reflect over the past year of relationships, asking the Holy Spirit to shine His light into any dark places in our hearts.

Yom Kippur, the holiest day of the year, was a day of commanded fasting. It was the only occasion when the priest wore white as He entered into the Holy of Holies to sprinkle the lamb's blood on the Mercy Seat, the place of deepest intimacy. This will be the day when the Supreme Ruler of the Universe, Jehovah *Elohim* will judge the nations and claim His bride. At the end of the day there is a very long shofar blast.

Remember that in a Jewish wedding the bridegroom also wears white. Could this be our wedding day? I don't know, it is yet another of the mysteries to be revealed. We don't know the day nor the hour. But we do know for sure: He is coming one day to claim His bride and we must be ready.

Next there are five days of quietness as we prepare for the most glorious feast of all, Tabernacles or *Sukkot*. This is celebrated by making a *sukka*, a temporary shelter outside and celebrating His presence with a feast for seven nights. (Note: Following the diaspora those outside of Jerusalem began to celebrate this feast for eight nights.) This reminds us that we too live in a temporary shelter, but one day we will dwell with Him forever more.

In studying and celebrating these feasts I have recognized the intricate attention to detail our Father has lavished on all of creation. He has spent thousands of years releasing the fullness of His covenant to us so that we might get a glimpse of His devotion, His passion, His love for us. He set the world in place and holds all things together by the power of His Word. Yet in His vast greatness, He has taken the time to plan every minute detail of each of our lives, insuring that we all are born with destiny, born with every available opportunity to walk in covenant with Him. Even the skies are not big enough to record all that He is nor all that we will be. There are still mysteries that we cannot fathom, untold treasures yet to be revealed.

But we do know this: He came to marry the widow, to claim His bride, His Other. We were intended as His bride from the very beginning of Creation. Even though we chose wrongly and fell, embracing death, and losing the glory essential to be a worthy partner for the King's Son, He made a way back for us.

Covenant.

He married the widow as the Great *Go'el*.

He is the Covenant Keeper.

Epilogue
Jesus, The Go'el, the Covenant Keeper

He is the King of the Universe rising with great splendor and judging the nations as all His enemies submit in reverence before Him.

He is awesome in majesty and brilliance and He rides on the wings of the wind.

He is the Commander of the angel armies warring to bring His Kingdom into the earth realm, securing your victory as His bride.

He is the Lion of the Tribe of Judah, thundering over the mountains roaring to establish His territory.

He is the sacrificial Lamb on the Cross with piercing fire in His eyes declaring, "This is for you, my bride."

Whether He is judging nations or fighting bloody wars, His heart and passion are focused toward a wedding. His wedding. From the beginning of time until the last trumpet blast, it has always been about His wedding. And about you, His pure spotless bride. Because He is the *Go'el*, the Covenant Keeper.

The Revelation of Jesus by John, the Disciple

Now I saw heaven opened, and behold, a white horse.
And He who sat on him was called Faithful and True…
His eyes were like a flame of fire, and on His head were many crowns.

I looked, and behold, in the midst of the throne stood a Lamb as though it had been slain. Then I looked, and I heard the voice of many angels around the throne, the living creatures, and the elders; and the number of them was ten thousand times ten thousand, and thousands of thousands, saying with a loud voice:

"Worthy is the Lamb who was slain
To receive power and riches and wisdom,
And strength and honor and glory and blessing!"

"Blessing and honor and glory and power
Be to Him who sits on the throne,
And to the Lamb, forever and ever!"

"Alleluia! For the Lord God Omnipotent reigns!
Let us be glad and rejoice and give Him glory,
for the marriage of the Lamb has come,
and His wife has made herself ready."
'Blessed are those who are called
To the marriage supper of the Lamb!

The Spirit and the bride say,
"Come!"

Works Referenced

Strong's Exhaustive Concordance of the Bible, James Strong. Electronic Edition STEP Files Copyright © 2005, QuickVerse.

Eastons Bible Dictionary: http://His.biblestudytools.com/dictionaries/eastons-bible-dictionary/covenant.html

"Covenant at Meal Time? The Real Deal Meal!" C. Merschbrock, https://ruthiespage.wordpress.com/2014/01/27/covenant-at-meal-time-the-real-deal-meal/ published Jan. 27, 2014.

Our Jubliee, Your Destiny, Charlotte Merschbrock, 2015.

"The Significance of Hittite Treaties for Biblical Studies and Orthodox Judaism," Yitzhaq Feder Ph.D., http://thetorah.com/significance-of-hittite-treaties-for-torah-judaism/

"The Two Tables of the Covenant," Meredith G. Kline, Westminster Theological Journal 22 (1960) 133-46. Copyright © 1960 by Westminster Theological Seminary. Cited with permission. http://His.meredithkline.com/files/articles/Kline-TwoTables-WTJ.pdf

Made in the USA
Columbia, SC
03 June 2019